W9-CCD-104

Reconstruction
and Reaction

Reconstruction and Reaction

THE EMANCIPATION OF SLAVES, 1861–1913

MICHAEL GOLAY

☑ Facts On File, Inc.
AN INFOBASE HOLDINGS COMPANY

Reconstruction and Reaction: The Emancipation of Slaves, 1861–1913

Facts On File, Inc.
11 Penn Plaza
New York NY 10001

Library of Congress Cataloging-in-Publication Data

Golay, Michael, 1951–
     Reconstruction and reaction : the emancipation of slaves, 1861–1913 / Michael Golay.
     p.   cm.—(Library of African-American history)
     Includes bibliographical references (p.   ) and index.
     Summary: Covers African-American advancements during the period of the federal government's management of the defeated Southern states.
     ISBN 0-8160-3318-8 (acid-free paper)
     1. Afro-Americans—History—1863–1877—Juvenil e literature.
     2. Afro-Americans—History—1877–1964—Juvenil e literature.
     3. Reconstruction—Juvenile literature. 4. Southern States—History—1865–1951—Juvenile literature. [1. Afro-Americans—History—1863–1877. 2. Afro-Americans—History—1877–1964. 3. Reconstruction.] I. Title. II. Series.
E185.2.G65 1996
975´.00496073—dc20   96-1881

Facts On File books are available at special discounts when purchased in bulk quantities for businesses, associations, institutions or sales promotions. Please call our Special Sales Department in New York at 212/967-8800 or 800/322-8755.

Text design by Catherine Rincon Hyman
Cover design by Nora Wertz
Illustrations by Dale Williams and Jeremy Eagle

This book is printed on acid-free paper.
Printed in the United States of America

MP FOF 10 9 8 7 6 5 4 3 2 1

Contents

Introduction

At the outset, America's leaders sought to fight the Civil War without reference to its primary cause, the enslavement of some 4 million people of African descent. Circumstances would force the issue, though—and sooner rather than later. To paraphrase the words of the abolitionist senator Charles Sumner, wherever one looked, one saw slavery.

A visionary few grasped this at once. "The Union's danger is the slave's deliverance," the *Anglo-African Weekly* announced in May 1861, only a month after the war broke out. "The idea may appear extravagant, and to the American mind repulsive, but we say that no adjustment of the nation's difficulty is possible until the claims of the black man are first met and satisfied."[1] The idea gradually took hold. And with the Emancipation Proclamation of January 1, 1863,

Abraham Lincoln transformed a war to repair the broken Union into a war of freedom for America's slaves.

This book examines the impact of war and emancipation on 19th-century African Americans. The narrative opens in November 1861, in Port Royal, South Carolina, where Union military power brought the first heady taste of freedom to plantation slaves of the Sea Islands. It ends in 1913, the 50th anniversary of the Emancipation Proclamation, when the Southern states lay in the grip of a relentless system of racial subordination and segregation.

Though the war brought emancipation, the struggle for freedom had only just begun. The era known as Reconstruction, roughly from 1865 to 1877, gave rise to all the issues for which African Americans would fight for a century and more: schools, economic opportunity and political power, and full rights of citizenship. These are issues of our own time, too. Poverty, lack of opportunity, and the corrosive effects of racism continue to afflict all too many descendants of the freed people of the 1860s.

The years of Reconstruction were confusing and chaotic for blacks and whites alike. They were also years of hope. Learning had been forbidden to slaves. With emancipation came schools; for the first time, tens of thousands of freed people of all ages were able to acquire the rudiments of an education. Slavery had robbed black people of their freedom of movement and of the fruits of their labor; emancipation gave them the chance to move from place to place in search of opportunity. It also offered former slaves their first experience of political power. Black men voted, sought and won elective office, and wrote and enforced laws.

The newfound opportunities did not last. Most Southern whites implacably opposed black advancement. With the war won and the Union restored, the Northern allies of the freed people lost interest in the cause. During the 1870s, white conservatives regained power, often by violent means, in state after state of the old Confederacy. They pushed blacks to the political, social, and economic margins, and kept them pinned there for generations.

So passed a historic opportunity to build a just multiracial society on the ruins of slavery. During the last years of the 19th century, the Southern states imposed the segregationist Jim Crow laws by which blacks were kept separate but never equal—a costly and socially destructive pattern that persisted almost unchanged in some places into the 1960s.

The system was as irrational as it was poisonous. In some communities, even the graveyards were segregated. In courts of law, whites and blacks swore on separate Bibles. In one South Carolina town, whites let it be known to blacks that the streets and shops were theirs on Saturday afternoons—but at no other time. "Those white folks didn't want you to come to town in the weekday at all," Mamie Garvin Fields recalled in the early 1980s. "Really, certain whites didn't like to think you had the leisure to do anything but pick cotton and work in the field."[2]

That, in fact, was far from the case. If the years of Reconstruction and reaction were in part a catalog of crimes, misdeeds, and neglect, they were also years of high achievement, gain, and hope. Many former slaves forged better, richer lives for themselves and their families. Black churches, schools and colleges, social organizations and businesses flourished.

All the same, Reconstruction failed to deliver the true full promise of emancipation into freedom. Part of the explanation is the lack of provision for the economic independence of freed people—which, in the 19th-century context, meant land reform and redistribution. Few former slaves had the wherewithal to become independent without government aid. So many remained bound to their former masters, working exhausted cottonlands for a bare subsistence.

The greatest failures, though, were not political or economic but moral. Americans lacked the vision and courage to ensure equality of opportunity, to enforce the law, to live up to their own best ideals. In falling short, the Reconstruction generation left a legacy of racial inequity and distrust that remains with us today.

NOTES

1. Leslie Fishel, Jr. and Benjamin Quarles, *The Black American: A Documentary History* (New York: William Morrow & Company, 1970), 220.

2. Edward L. Ayers, *The Promise of the New South: Life After Reconstruction* (New York: Oxford University Press, 1992), 132.

Chronology

April 12–14, 1861
The Confederate attack on Fort Sumter, S.C. touches off the Civil War.

November 7, 1861
Union forces take possession of Port Royal Sound, S.C. The federal occupation means freedom for several thousand African-American slaves.

March 1862
The first contingent of Northern abolitionists known as the Gideonites reaches the Port Royal area of South Carolina and begins the program of education, wage labor, and land reform to be known as the Port Royal Experiment.

May 1862
General David Hunter begins a campaign to recruit former slaves for the Union army.

September 22, 1862

After the battle of Antietam, a Union victory, President Lincoln issues the preliminary Emancipation Proclamation, which declares that slaves in the rebellious states will be free on January 1, 1863.

November 1862

The First South Carolina Volunteers, a regiment of freed slaves, is mustered into the Union army at Beaufort, S.C.

January 1, 1863

President Lincoln issues the Emancipation Proclamation.

January–July 1863

Union military operations in Mississippi free thousands of slaves. Many work as wage laborers for General Ulysses S. Grant's army.

April 8, 1864

Senate passes the Fourteenth Amendment to the Constitution, which formally abolishes slavery in the United States and its territories.

November–December 1864

General William T. Sherman's march from Atlanta to the sea liberates thousands of Georgia slaves. Sherman tries to persuade the freed people to remain home, but many follow the army anyway. Over the winter, the Sherman refugees experience great hardship.

1865

Wisconsin, Connecticut, and Minnesota deny the vote to blacks.

Mid-January 1865

Sherman issues Special Orders No. 15, reserving the coastal region of Georgia and South Carolina for the settlement of the freed people.

March 3, 1865

Congress establishes the Bureau of Refugees, Freedmen and Abandoned Lands—the Freedmen's Bureau—to provide aid to former slaves and others the war has displaced or impoverished.

April 9, 1865

The main Confederate field army surrenders at Appomattox Court House, Va., and within weeks the Civil War is brought to a close.

April 14–15, 1865

John Wilkes Booth mortally wounds President Lincoln at Ford's Theater in Washington. On the death of Lincoln, Andrew Johnson becomes president.

Summer 1865

Tensions build between blacks and whites as paroled Confederate soldiers arrive home. Former slaves resist pressure to agree to labor arrangements binding them to low-paid field work for their former masters.

September 1865

Journalist/politician Carl Schurz reports on crisis conditions in the South as unrepentant Confederates return to power. President Johnson ignores Schurz's conclusion that federal authority is necessary to protect the freed people's rights.

December 1865

President Johnson declares Reconstruction complete. Most Southern states deny even limited political rights to former slaves. "Black Codes" in Mississippi and other states sharply restrict blacks' freedom.

December 1865

The Thirteenth Amendment abolishing slavery is ratified.

February–March 1866

Congress passes a civil rights bill and a measure extending the life of the Freedmen's Bureau. President Johnson vetoes both bills; both vetoes are overridden.

1866

Fisk Free School is established in Nashville, Tenn. In 1871, it will become Fisk University—one of the great black institutions of higher learning.

June 1866

Congress approves the Fourteenth Amendment, which extends full citizenship rights to former slaves.

November 1866

In the autumn elections, Radical Republicans strengthen their hold on Congress, setting the stage for a showdown with President Johnson over Reconstruction.

March 3, 1867

Congress passes the First Reconstruction Act over Johnson's veto. It divides the South into five military districts and authorizes the U.S. Army to enroll voters to elect state conventions that will draw up constitutions guaranteeing black political rights.

May 1867

Ku Klux Klan groups begin a systematic terror campaign against black political activists and their Northern allies.

February 24, 1868

House of Representatives votes to impeach President Johnson, mainly for impeding congressional Reconstruction of the former Confederate states.

May 26, 1868

By one vote, the Senate fails to convict Johnson and remove him from office.

November 1868
With overwhelming support from newly enfranchised blacks, Ulysses S. Grant wins the presidency.

February 1869
Congress proposes a Fifteenth Amendment to the Constitution that would guarantee voting rights to every male citizen regardless of race or previous condition of servitude.

January 1870
The Mississippi legislature elects Hiram Revels to the U.S. Senate; Revels becomes the first African American to serve in either house of Congress.

February 1870
The Fifteenth Amendment is ratified and becomes law.

May 1870
Reacting to Ku Klux Klan violence, Congress passes the first of the Enforcement Acts mandating heavy penalties for interfering with a citizen's right to vote.

November 1872
President Grant is reelected. He again draws substantial black support.

1875
Blanche K. Bruce of Mississippi takes his seat in the U.S. Senate. In 1881, he becomes the only black to serve a full Senate term until the middle of the 20th century.

March 1875
Congress approves a Civil Rights Act guaranteeing all citizens equal access to public facilities such as railroad trains, restaurants, and hotels.

November 1875
After a murderous campaign of intimidation, Democrats win majorities in both houses of the Mississippi legislature, thus "redeeming" the state for conservative whites.

March 2, 1877

Republican Rutherford B. Hayes is declared the winner of the disputed presidential election of 1876. In return for Southern support, he agrees to withdraw the last federal troops from the South and abandon federal efforts to safeguard black rights.

April 10, 1877

Hayes resolves the disputed South Carolina election in favor of Democrat Wade Hampton and orders U.S. troops to withdraw from the state. Two weeks later, Hayes withdraws the last federal troops from the Louisiana statehouse in Baton Rouge, guaranteeing exclusively white rule there.

Spring 1879

In a spontaneous movement, thousands of blacks migrate northwest in search of land and freedom—the famous "Exodusters."

1881

Black activist Frederick Douglass publishes the final revision of his autobiography, titled *Life and Times of Frederick Douglass.*

1883

The U.S. Supreme Court rules the 1875 Civil Rights Act unconstitutional.

1884

John R. Lynch is elected temporary chairman of the Republican National Convention, the first African American to preside over a national political gathering.

1887

Florida enacts the first Jim Crow law. Segregationist legislation soon regulates every aspect of Southern life.

1893

George Murray of South Carolina is the only black to be seated in the 53rd Congress.

1894

W. E. B. DuBois is the first African American to be awarded a Ph.D. degree from Harvard.

September 18, 1895

Booker T. Washington delivers his famous "Atlanta Compromise" speech, which seems to call for accommodation with white views on race.

1896

In *Plessy v. Ferguson*, the U.S. Supreme Court validates the "separate but equal" doctrine of Southern racial segregation. The ruling stands until 1954.

1905

Black scholar, author and activist W. E. B. DuBois helps launch the Niagara Movement, which challenges accommodationists such as Booker T. Washington and demands equal rights for blacks.

1913

Black communities across the nation mark the 50th anniversary of the Emancipation Proclamation.

1

War and Freedom: 1861–1863

Many years after the event, the Sea Island people remembered November 7, 1861 as "the day of the big gun-shoot." The great guns belonged to 17 warships of the United States Navy, and they were turned that autumn morning on the two Confederate forts guarding the entrance to Port Royal Sound, South Carolina. After a four-hour bombardment, the defenders fled and several thousand U.S. troops came ashore. At a single stroke, the Union gained control of one of the finest natural harbors on the South Atlantic coast, an ideal anchorage and coaling station for the squadrons clamping a blockade on Confederate seaports.

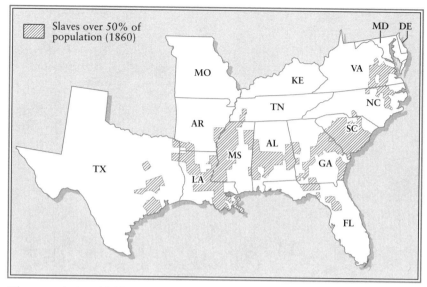

Slave population, 1860.

The white planters of the South Carolina Sea Islands retreated too, leaving behind a bumper crop of valuable long-staple cotton almost ready for shipment. The islands—part of a chain along the South Carolina and Georgia Coast—were thus left in the possession of some 10,000 African-American slaves who, aware of what the guns were saying, refused to follow their masters onto the mainland. When federal troops entered Beaufort, the chief town of the Sea Islands, on November 8, they encountered only a single representative of the planter class. He evidently had been too drunk to respond to the alarm and take himself away.

On the plantations, the enslaved people responded to the departure of their overseers by setting fire to cotton gins and other symbols of cotton culture. They ransacked storehouses and plantation mansions. In abandoned Beaufort, they looted planters' town houses. Arriving Union troops found furniture and broken glass in piles in the sandy streets. The federals were surprised to discover how few slaves actually had gone off with their masters. "It was with difficulty they could get away with a household domestic—the field hands remained to a man," reported Flag Officer Samuel F. DuPont, commander of the invasion fleet.[1] Jubilant blacks crowded around the landing parties, cheering the U.S. flag.

Though the Sea Islanders could not yet be certain of it, the U.S. armed forces represented freedom. Conceived as a military operation, Port Royal evolved into the first large-scale experiment in emancipation—what the historian Willie Lee Rose has called a "rehearsal for reconstruction." Some of the first black U.S. soldiers were recruited from among former slaves in the coastal lowlands. Here were the first schools and the first efforts to distribute land to the freed people. Here, too, freedmen had their first experience of democratic politics.

Still, only the vaguest outline of what would come to be known as the Port Royal Experiment could be discerned in November 1861. Before the South could be reconstructed, the Civil War had to be won. As President Lincoln had repeatedly asserted, the North was waging war solely to restore the federal union. "My paramount object in this struggle is to save the Union and is not either to save or destroy slavery," Lincoln said.[2] In the North, abolition had grown in the 1850s into the greatest protest movement of the century. The political conflict over the extension of slavery had touched off the Civil War. But in the war's first phase, at least, slavery and freedom were no part of the federal cause.

The *coerced* labor of people of African origin dated back to the earliest period of European settlement of North America. The first enslaved Africans landed in Virginia in the 1620s. With the gradual advance of the frontier, the institution spread south and west. Slaves raised the great Southern cash crops—first tobacco, later cotton and rice.

The Northern states outlawed slavery during and just after the American Revolution. In the South, a powerful ruling class that depended on slavery sought to preserve the institution as much for political and social as for economic reasons. During the first decades of the 19th century, the industrial revolution gave new life and new value to slavery. Slaves cultivated the cotton that fed the looms and spindles that enriched the North. And while New England industrialists carried on a profitable business with King Cotton, New England moralists led the crusade for the abolition of slavery.

At mid-century, the slave population approached 4 million, the majority of whom lived in the Deep South, though many thousands of slaves lived in the border states of Delaware, Maryland, Kentucky, and Missouri. About a quarter of all Southern white families owned slaves, though most were smallholders: 90 percent of slaveholders owned fewer than 20 slaves. Some 10,000 families made up the so-called planter aristocracy, only about a third of which owned more than 100 slaves.

Treatment of slaves varied widely. They could not, of course, move about at will, own land, or obtain an education. Slaves were valuable property, so quite apart from humane considerations planters had an incentive to see that they were adequately fed and sheltered. Slaves put in long days at hard labor for a subsistence. A slave cost the master $19 a year, the African-American historian W. E. B. DuBois estimated; enslaved people were therefore "among the poorest paid laborers in the modern world."[3] A former field hand in the rich Red River bottomlands of Arkansas recalled going into the cotton fields at first light and working straight through until dark, with only a single 10- or 15-minute break at noon. When there was a full moon, work continued deep into the night. Toil, a monotonous diet, and exposure to winter chills and damps took a long-term toll on slaves' health. Fewer than five of every hundred lived beyond their 60th birthday.

The sectional crisis—the political, economic, social, and moral gulf that divided North and South—deepened during the 1850s. The principle of free labor and free soil in the Western territories brought about the birth of a new political

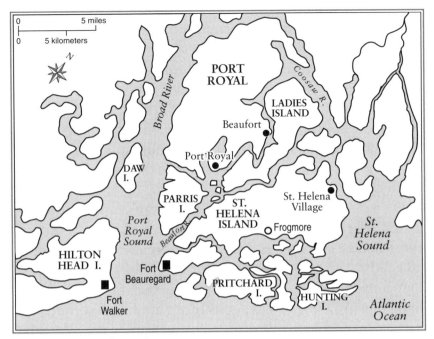

Sea Islands, South Carolina.

organization, the Republican Party, during the middle years of the decade. After the Illinois Republican Abraham Lincoln won the presidency in a four-way election in November 1860, the Southern slave states began, one after another, to secede. By the spring of 1861, 11 slave states had come together to form the Confederacy. When Confederate forces opened fire on Union-held Fort Sumter, South Carolina, on April 12, the North went to war to force the rebellious states to return to the union.

Initially, Lincoln directed U.S. military forces not to interfere with established institutions in the South. In practice, nearly every slave and even some masters understood that, sooner or later, emancipation would become the chief issue of the war. A North Carolina planter put the case plainly to his slaves. "There is a war commenced between the North and the South," he explained. "If the North whups, you will be as free a man as I is. If the South whups, you will be a slave all your days."[4] The appearance of federal troops, enslaved people came to learn, meant the certain approach of freedom.

Wartime circumstances required rough and ready policies for dealing with fugitives and refugees. Within a few months of the outbreak of fighting, thousands of slaves had run away from their masters and sought protection by federal troops. Union commanders in the field found they would either have to reinterpret Lincoln's noninterference directive or ignore it entirely.

In one famous and absurd incident in the summer of 1861, a Confederate officer appeared under a flag of truce to ask the federals at Fortress Monroe, Virginia to return three escaped slaves to him. The federal commander, General Benjamin F. Butler, refused, declaring the fugitives contraband of war. While runaways were not actually to be set free, neither were they to be sent back to their owners. In fact, Butler drafted many former slaves as Union army laborers. In the jargon of the time, slaves without masters became known as contrabands.

The senior commanders at Port Royal confronted the issue in November and December 1861. Brigadier General Thomas W. Sherman, the army commander, posted the obligatory proclamation promising that social and local institutions (meaning slavery) would be left undisturbed. In the low country, though, it was the masters who had run off. Somehow, Sea Island society had to be organized along new lines. There were contraband human beings; there were warehouses full of contraband cotton. On orders from Washington, Sherman set about trying to hire former slaves to gather, process, and pack cotton for shipment north.

At around the same time, Lincoln's treasury secretary, Salmon P. Chase, hit on the idea of authorizing government agents to collect contraband cotton and sell it, with the proceeds to help pay for the Union effort. At year's end, Chase resolved to take the project a step further. He assigned Edward L. Pierce, a Massachusetts lawyer with abolitionist leanings, to go to Port Royal to organize an African-American labor force and get a cotton crop into the ground for 1862.

Reaching Hilton Head Island in mid-January, Pierce set immediately to work. In a report to Secretary Chase, he recommended appointing Northern superintendents to manage the abandoned cotton plantations. The local people (no longer slaves yet not altogether free) were to return to their old plantation tasks. They would be paid wages. Whipping and other relics of slavery times were to be prohibited. Pierce also recommended approaching Northern charitable organizations to provide missionaries to teach in schools to be established for former slaves.

In response, and with impressive speed, a legion of Northern missionaries, teachers, labor reformers and other high-minded persons known as Gideon's Band mobilized for action in the South Carolina Sea Islands. "You don't know what a satisfaction it is to feel at last that there is a chance for me to *do something* in this great work which is going on," wrote Edward Philbrick, the engineer son of a prominent Massachusetts abolitionist, who not only volunteered to come south with the Gideonites but made an out-of-pocket contribution of $1,000 to the cause.[5]

The advance party, 41 men and 12 women, all white, sailed from New York to Hilton Head on the steamer *Atlantic* in early March 1862. A thin, freezing rain fell out of a leaden sky. The Gideonites passed the dreary hours singing Methodist hymns. Observing the others, Philbrick wondered whether his enthusiasm had perhaps been misplaced. "We have a rather motley-looking set," he wrote of his fellow volunteers. "A good many look like broken-down school-masters or ministers who have excellent dispositions but not much talent. I don't believe there will be a great deal of cotton raised under their superintendence."[6] Nor were Philbrick's first impressions of the Sea Islands favorable. Hilton Head stretched long, low and sandy, a drab, flat landscape broken only by occasional sand hills. A doubtful-looking wharf had been built for the steamers. Army camps and storehouses straggled for a mile or more along the bank of the Broad River.

Things looked more promising ashore. Pierce gave Philbrick responsibility for Thomas Coffin's plantation on St. Helena Island, the largest in the district with some 250 hands in prewar times. Here and on two smaller plantations in his charge, Pierce expected to carry out a free labor experiment that would uplift the Sea Islanders and earn handsome cotton profits besides.

The low-country spring felt sweet after the icy drizzle of the North Atlantic. The sun shone warm; peach and orange trees were in fragrant blossom. Still, necessities of all kinds were lacking. Conditions in the slave quarters were primitive. "There being no water power and no steam," Philbrick observed, "every negro grinds his peck of corn in a handmill as in the year one." [7] In a letter to his wife Helen, who would soon join him on St. Helena, he recommended packing at least three umbrellas, flypaper, tin cups, bowls, a teapot, wooden boxes for rice and sugar, a knife, fork and spoon, and a thermometer.

If the engineer Philbrick personified hard-headed Yankee business efficiency, Laura Towne, a Philadelphia abolitionist with training in homeopathic medicine, seemed to embody Northern sincerity and good will. "We have come to do anti-slavery work, and we think it noble work and mean to do it earnestly," Towne announced on arrival at Hilton Head on April 9. [8] Nominally a secretary/housekeeper at Philbrick's headquarters, she soon sought out extra work, distributing charitable donations of food and clothing among the former slaves, dispensing medicine, and, eventually, teaching school.

In Philbrick's view, careful business management and the unfettered play of market forces were the keys to the transition from bondage to freedom. Charity would hardly be

South Carolina slaves return from the cotton fields with the day's harvest in 1860. Freed people resisted pressure to return to the fields as wage laborers, viewing cotton as the "slave crop." (New-York Historical Society)

sufficient, and in any case, he thought, Sea Islanders were quick to sense the limits of Northern tenderheartedness. "If you feel any hesitation about coming in contact with them you shouldn't come," he had advised his wife, "for they are sharp enough to detect apathy or lurking repugnance, which would render any amount of theoretical sympathy about worthless."[9] Philbrick correctly gauged some Gideonites as ineffective, paternalistic, and burdened with racist assumptions. Few if any had the intelligence, commitment or stamina of Laura Towne, who made the Sea Islands her life's work, staying on until her death in 1901.

From the beginning, there were conflicts among the soldiers, missionaries, and freed people. The soldiers regarded the volunteers as incompetent and fuzzy-minded. The Gideonites found the soldiers overbearing, autocratic and, sometimes, corrupt. The Sea Islanders, an exotic people, so long isolated from mainland South Carolina that they spoke a strange dialect all their own (one that was all but incomprehensible to outsiders), were suspicious and mistrustful of all whites, especially the soldiers. They complained that the Yankee troops stole their livestock and broke up their fences for firewood, and that the Gideonite superintendents could think only of how much low-wage field work they could sweat out of them.

Towne aligned herself with the radical wing of the Gideonites. The Reverend Mansfield French, a New York abolitionist, best expressed this group's creed: "God's programme," he said, "involves freedom in its largest sense—free soil, free schools, free ballot boxes, free representation."[10] For Philbrick and his allies, the paramount issues were the free labor experiment, cotton, and profits. With these, everything else would fall into place soon enough. Free labor would produce more cotton than slave labor had produced. The freed people, with cash in their pockets, would form a large new market for Northern goods. The result: progress and prosperity for all.

So went the theory. In practice, however, many blacks resisted cultivating cotton, which they called "the slave crop." In mid-December, General Sherman reported that only 60 or so able-bodied males had responded to his call for laborers to prepare the 1861 cotton crop for shipment. By contrast, Union officers found Sea Islanders nearly always ready to help with other tasks. "They assisted us voluntarily whenever we wanted their aid, and I overheard one of them say that it was fair that they should do so for us, as we were working for them," Navy commander Percival Drayton noted.[11]

Cotton, however, proved another matter. Philbrick's free labor harangues failed to inspire the workers. "The Yankees preach nothing but cotton, cotton!" one black parson complained.[12] Nor could the old expedient of physical abuse—beatings, whipping—be used. William Gannett, who came to Port Royal to teach but found plantation management a more congenial employment, confessed one day that he had lost his temper and struck a recalcitrant field hand, knocking him to the ground. Day after day, he complained, he had difficulty getting the ex-slaves to work.

Perceptive whites grasped the cause of this reluctance to return to the old plantation tasks. Blacks suspected that however much wealth cotton brought, little of it would be likely to trickle down to them. For anyone who cared to listen, Sea Islanders were perfectly clear about what they wanted: land, schools, and the vote. When Philbrick at last abandoned the gang labor system of slavery days and decided to "throw each family on its own responsibility, allowing them to choose their own time and manner of working" the land, he obtained much better results.[13] The freed people considered the plots to be their own property, in which they had a direct stake.

Towne and others could see, too, that slavery had been the worst of schools for freedom. Slavery taught dependency and accommodation. It punished initiative and independent thought. Perversely, the system rewarded shirking, malingering, lying and thievery. Forms of passive resistance, these were also means of making everyday existence slightly more tolerable. Otherwise sympathetic whites complained

Slave dwellings were grouped together in so-called slave quarters such as this one on Mill's Plantation, Port Royal Island, S.C. With freedom, many families scattered, preferring to build new cabins nearer to the fields they worked. (Library of Congress)

constantly of former slaves' seeming lack of respect for private property. Sea Islanders had another view. "They take all our labor, and steal our children, and we only take their chicken," one responded.[14] Often, what whites defined as theft looked to freed people like long-delayed compensation for years of forced labor.

Even when they meant well, Union soldiers could be as uncomprehending as Edward Pierce's cotton superintendents.

In late March 1862, Major General David Hunter, a regular officer with abolitionist views, replaced Thomas Sherman in command of the Port Royal region. In early April, he formally declared some ex-slaves free. On May 9, he issued a general emancipation proclamation covering all the enslaved people in his department, which comprised South Carolina, Georgia, and Florida.

On his own authority, Hunter launched an army recruiting drive among blacks. He met with little success. Young men disappeared into the swamps at the first sight of the recruiters. Frederick Douglass and other free African-American leaders were campaigning hard for black enlistments, but Sea Islanders knew little of this. "They do not yet realize that they have a country to fight for," Pierce explained. Hunter persisted, however. Over the protests of the cotton superintendents, he sent squads of white soldiers out to the plantations to forcibly draft young black men and carry them off to Hilton Head for military training. This made a bad situation worse. "They think it is a trap to get the able-bodied and send them to Cuba to sell," Towne noted.[15] In prewar times, Hilton Head had been a departure point for American slaves sold into the Caribbean.

Pursuing his cautious, conservative policy, Lincoln revoked Hunter's emancipation order. The president also discouraged Hunter's efforts to raise a legion of black troops. The government actually refused to pay the 150 or so former slaves Hunter had managed to enlist, forcing him finally to give up the effort.

While the freed people resisted the cotton superintendents and the army recruiters, they responded with enthusiasm to the schoolteachers. Since 1740, it had been a crime in South Carolina to teach enslaved people to write. In 1862, former slaves, more than 95 percent of whom were illiterate, enrolled as fast as schools could be opened. By May, the school at the Coffin Point plantation had 138 students, nearly half of them adult field hands. The school in Beaufort had 100 students. In September, Laura Towne and her companion Ellen Murray opened a school at Frogmore on St. Helena Island. By year's end 2,500 former slaves, adults and children alike, were being taught in 30 schools in the Port Royal area.

Towne, Mansfield French, and other radical Gideonites strongly endorsed Sea Islanders' dreams of owning land. Abandoned plantations could be subdivided, with plots sold to blacks on generous terms or even granted free to encourage independence and self-sufficiency. Here again, the radicals came into conflict with Philbrick and the cotton superintendents. When the government offered rebel property for sale in early 1863, Philbrick and his group of Boston investors bought 11 plantations totaling 8,000 acres and containing a population of around 1,000 freed people. The intent, of course, was to raise high-quality cotton employing blacks as wage laborers. But families growing their own subsistence crops on their own land were hardly likely to agree to work for Philbrick. Pooling their resources, groups of former slaves managed to buy up about 2,000 acres for themselves.

The Port Royal experiment played itself out during the spring and summer of 1862 against a backdrop of Union military reverses. Federal defeats in Virginia cast a pall over the Sea Islands. With several of his regiments sent north to reinforce the Army of the Potomac, Hunter withdrew the federal garrison from outlying Edisto Island, inviting the old masters to return. In September, though, a ray of hope burned through the gloom. Lincoln used the occasion of the battle at Antietam Creek in Maryland to issue a preliminary Emancipation Proclamation, that declared that slaves would be free from January 1, 1863 onwards. All at once, Lincoln's action converted the war for restoration of the Union into an antislavery crusade.

Lincoln had always been ambivalent about slavery. His attitudes, like those of most 19th-century whites, were frankly racist. Lincoln opposed the westward extension of

Soldiers of the 107th U.S. Colored Troops on guard detail at Fort Corcoran near Washington, D.C. Senator Charles Sumner of Massachusetts fought for equal treatment for black troops, who were paid less than white enlistees. In 1865–66, Sumner fought for the right of these black veterans to vote. (Library of Congress)

slavery in the 1850s, but he had no desire at that time to attack the institution in the regions where it had long existed. By mid-1862, it seemed certain that the war would bring about the destruction of slavery. That, Lincoln thought, would raise an entirely new set of questions.

"You and we are different races," the president told a group of African-American leaders in 1862. "We have between us a broader difference than exists between almost any other two races. Your race suffers very greatly by living among us, while ours suffers from your presence. In a word, we suffer on each side. It is better for us both, therefore, to be separated."[16]

Lincoln, in fact, favored the resettlement of freed slaves elsewhere, possibly in islands in the Caribbean or in Africa.

Failing that, he believed there would have to be some form of racial subordination. The historian Kenneth M. Stampp summed up Lincoln's views on the eve of emancipation this way: "The Negroes, if they remained, would be governed by the white men among whom they lived, subject only to certain minimum requirements of fair play."[17]

Military necessity forced Lincoln to reconsider his views on the recruitment of blacks. Congress endorsed the raising of black regiments in mid-1862; in late August the secretary of war, Edwin Stanton, authorized the army at Port Royal to enlist and train as many as 5,000 black volunteers. Enlistees would be certified as free, and so would their wives, mothers, and children.

As in the spring, recruiting went slowly at first. Few Sea Islanders volunteered, though they showed no hesitation about defending their homes. For months, they had been serving as scouts and informal pickets. On the night of October 23, a detachment of armed blacks on St. Helena Island, acting on their own, drove off two boatloads of Confederate raiders. Yet on the same night, not a single black male of military age turned up for a recruitment meeting on St. Helena.

"The negroes reindicate their claim to humanity by shirking the draft in every possible way, acting exactly like *white men* under similar circumstances," a sympathetic Union officer wrote.[18] Still, by November, sufficient numbers had enlisted to form a regiment of freed slaves: the First South Carolina Volunteers. They were the first of more than 130,000 former slaves to be recruited from the Confederate states.

Black troops served in all-black units under white officers. They were paid less than white enlistees—$10 a month compared to $13 a month. The First South Carolina Volunteers had a further $3 a month deducted for clothing. In protest, some of the men refused to accept the monthly balance of $7. "We give our soldiering to the Government, Colonel," one man told Bostonian Thomas Wentworth

Higginson, the regimental commander, "but we won't despise ourselves so much for to take the seven dollar." Still, inequalities aside, many enlistees realized they had crossed a threshhold of freedom. Said ex-slave Thomas Long of the First South Carolina:

> If we hadn't become soldiers, all might have gone back as it was before; our freedom might have slipped through the two houses of Congress and President Lincoln's four years might have passed and nothing been done for us. But now things can never go back, because we have showed our energy and courage and our natural manhood.[19]

President Lincoln signed the Emancipation Proclamation late in the afternoon of January 1, 1863. Reflecting Lincoln's political circumspection and his ambivalence about the war's purpose, the proclamation excluded some 450,000 slaves in the loyal border states, another 275,000 in Union-held Tennessee, and thousands more in Union-occupied portions of Virginia and Louisiana. As for the rest, the more than 3 million slaves in the Confederate states, they "are and henceforth shall be free," the president declared.

The news spread through the slave quarters of the Confederate South, though most slaves thought it prudent to keep their knowledge of the event to themselves. "Oh, yes, massa," a Virginia slave told a Northern parson later in 1863, "we all know about it, only we darsn't let on. We pretend not to know."[20] But in their camp near Beaufort, the First South Carolina Volunteers celebrated openly with a dress parade, a picnic, speeches and singing.

Years later, Charlotte Forten, a freeborn African American from Philadelphia who had come to Beaufort to teach, recalled that bright, mild New Year's Day when Lincoln's words were read aloud to gatherings of thousands of former slaves. "It all seemed like a brilliant dream," she wrote.[21]

The Power of the "Praise House"_____

Religion played a powerful role in the lives of enslaved people. Many masters encouraged the practice of Christianity, often taking on responsibility for seeing to their slaves' spiritual well-being. Sometimes, though, religious observances were secret, hidden from overseer and master—an important emotional and intellectual outlet and even, on occasion, a form of resistance to slavery.

"In great measure," noted the Gideonite William Channing Gannett in explaining the appeal of religion to the freed people of South Carolina's Sea Islands, "it takes the place of social entertainment and amusements."[22]

Sea Islanders practiced their religion with an intensity that seemed strange, even disturbing, to the white missionaries who worked among them during the 1860s. "They all believe in hell!" teacher Mary Ames remarked.[23] African Americans called their informal plantation churches "praise houses." Their, vivid, colorful, demonstrative services ended

NOTES

1. Willie Lee Rose, *Rehearsal for Reconstruction: The Port Royal Experiment* (Indianapolis: Bobbs, Merrill, 1964), 107.

2. Kenneth M. Stampp, *The Era of Reconstruction, 1865–1877* (New York: Alfred A. Knopf, 1965), 44.

3. W. E. B. DuBois, *Black Reconstruction in America* (New York: Russell & Russell, 1962), 9.

4. Leon F. Litwack, *Been in the Storm So Long: The Aftermath of Slavery* (New York: Alfred A. Knopf, 1979), 5.

5. Rose, *Rehearsal for Reconstruction*, 50.

6. Elizabeth Ware Pearson, ed., *Letters from Port Royal, 1862–1868* (New York: Arno Press, 1969 reprint edition), 2.

7. Rose, *Rehearsal for Reconstruction*, 157.

8. Pearson, ed., *Letters from Port Royal*, ii.

with a "Shout"—a form of dance, wild and energetic, usually to the repetitious singing of a familiar hymn. Some of the Gideonites were, to put it plainly, shocked—even the tolerant, accepting Laura Towne. "I never saw anything so savage," she said.[24]

Black churches were simple, makeshift, and plain. Northern journalist Whitelaw Reid visited one in Louisiana that doubled as a dormitory. A double cabin with the center partition knocked out, it could accommodate a family of five as well as the entire congregation. There were few trappings, though Reid did make a note of the wall decorations—likenesses of Abraham Lincoln and his son Tad, General Grant, and, inexplicably, Confederate general Joseph E. Johnston.

The preacher, Reid discovered, had been pulled from his pulpit during slavery times and whipped "for presuming to repeat passages of the Bible, and talk about them to the slaves."[25] When he recovered, he resumed his preaching—and his habit of quoting from biblical texts.

Such courage perhaps explains the preachers' tremendous power, influence, and prestige in black communities. A black preacher, the historian W. E. B. DuBois wrote, served as "a leader, a politician, an orator, a 'boss,' an intriguer, an idealist."[26] ◆

9. Pearson, ed., *Letters from Port Royal*, 11.

10. Rose, *Rehearsal for Reconstruction*, 218.

11. *Official Record of the Union and Confederate Navies in the War of the Rebellion*, Series 1, Volume 12 (Washington: U.S. Government, 1901), 294.

12. Laura M. Towne, *The Letters and Diary of Laura M. Towne*, Rupert M. Holland, ed. (New York: Negro Universities Press, 1969 reprint), 20.

13. Towne, *Letters and Diary*, 19.

14. Litwack, *Been in the Storm*, 143.

15. First quote, *Official Record of the War of the Rebellion*, Series 3, Volume 2 (Washington: U.S. Government, 1899), 56; second quote, Towne, *Letters and Diary*, 37.

16. Stampp, *Era of Reconstruction*, 35.

17. Stampp, *Era of Reconstruction*, 48.

18. Litwack, *Been in the Storm*, 75.

19. First quote, Thomas W. Higginson, *Army Life in A Black Regiment* (New York: Collier Books, 1962 reprint), 245; second quote, Litwack, *Been in the Storm*, 102.

20. Litwack, *Been in the Storm*, 19.

21. Charlotte Forten, *The Journal of Charlotte Forten*, Ray A. Billington, ed. (New York: W. W. Norton, 1981), 171–72.

22. Rose, *Rehearsal for Reconstruction*, 93.

23. Mary Ames, *A New England Woman's Diary in Dixie* (New York: Negro Universities Press, 1969 reprint), 68.

24. Rose, *Rehearsal for Reconstruction*, 93.

25. Whitelaw Reid, *After the War: A Tour of the Southern States, 1865–1866*, C. Vann Woodward, ed. (New York: Harper & Row, 1965), 524.

26. Edward L. Ayers, *The Promise of the New South: Life after Reconstruction* (New York: Oxford University Press, 1992), 164.

2

"Forty Acres and a Mule": 1862–1865

$$F$$reedom came sooner
for some, later for others. Only the power of the Union army
could transform Lincoln's Emancipation Proclamation from
vision to reality. Federal forces occupied New Orleans and
its environs in the spring of 1862, breaking up the slave
system in those regions. In the summer of 1863, a Union
army under Ulysses S. Grant captured the Confederate fortress of Vicksburg on the Mississippi, opening the great river
from St. Louis to the Gulf of Mexico and freeing tens of
thousands of enslaved people. Late in 1864, William T.
Sherman carried out his destructive, liberating march
through Georgia to the sea.

In some places, freedom came without warning. "We're
digging potatoes when the Yankees came up with two big

wagons and make us come out of the fields and freed us," a Louisiana slave remembered. "There wasn't no celebration about it. Massa says we can stay a couple days till we decide what to do."[1]

Abrupt change of such magnitude could be as confusing as it was inspiriting. Recalled a Virginia slave:

> It came so sudden on them they wasn't prepared for it. Just think of whole droves of people, that had always been kept so close, and hardly ever left the plantation before, turned loose all at once, with nothing in the world but what they had on their backs, and often little enough of that; men, women and children that had left their homes when they found out they were free, walking along the road with nowhere to go.[2]

At first, Grant's Western army showed little inclination to recognize the enormous social consequences of its battlefield victories. There were few precedents. Resources were limited. The freed people, the soldiers seemed to think, could shift for themselves. "Old and young, sick and well, they were turned loose to the open sky, naked to their enemies," Frederick Douglass said. In contested areas, African Americans sometimes found themselves caught between two fires. "One night there'd be a gang of Secesh [Confederates], and the next one, there'd come along a gang of Yankees," a Louisiana man recalled. "Pa was afraid of both of 'em. Secesh said they'd kill him if he left his white folks. Yankees said they'd kill him if he didn't leave 'em."[3]

In Mississippi, only about half the state's 500,000 slaves were free by war's end. On some remote plantations, masters and overseers simply refused to accept emancipation, even after federal forces had arrived in the vicinity. Sometimes, as a last attempt to exercise his fast-disappearing authority, a master would call the enslaved people together to explain the

Refugees ford the Rappahannock River in Virginia in the aftermath of Union general John Pope's retreat from Manassas in August 1862. For tens of thousands of slaves, freedom depended on the success of the federal armies. (Library of Congress)

changed circumstances. A Mississippi freedman quoted his former owner:

> Sit down there all of you and listen to what I got to tell you. I hate to do it but I must. You all ain't my niggers no more. You is free. Just as free as I am. Here I have raised you all to work for me, and now you are going to leave me. I am an old man, and I can't get along without you. I don't know what I am going to do.[4]

In fact, as Douglass had suggested, a mutual dependency bound many masters and slaves. Some well-treated slaves, especially house servants, were ambivalent about the collapse of the old order and apprehensive about the future. "I was a-farin' pretty well in the kitchen," a favored servant named Aleck Trimble told a Northern interviewer. "I ain't never felt like a bond slave what's been pressed—that's what them soldiers say we all are," remarked a Florida woman.

Many slaves, too, had unreasonable expectations. A popular chant ran:

> Hurrah, hurrah for freedom!
> It makes the head spin 'roun'
> The nigger in the saddle
> And the white man on the groun'.[5]

A young South Carolina slave named Margaret Hughes approached an aunt with her fears about the coming of the Yankees. What, she wanted to know, would become of her? "Child, we going to have such a good time a settin' at the white folks' table, and a rocking in the big rocking chair," Margaret's aunt assured her.[6]

After the initial shock of freedom, former slaves confronted danger, hardship, and want. The Yankees, all too many learned, could be a thieving and rapacious set of liberators. The freed people could be as resentful as their former masters of Yankee plundering. "We helped raise that meat they stole," a Mississippi man said. "They left us to starve and fed their fat selves on what was our living."[7] Sometimes, the federals stole directly from storehouses in the slave quarters.

While some Northerners had gone into the war as convinced abolitionists, the racial views of many Union soldiers were hardly more advanced than those of their enemies. "I dont think enough of the Niggar to go and fight for them," an Ohio soldier wrote just before he enlisted. "I would rather fight them." Still, few Yankees, however racist their views, were unmoved by the first evidence of slavery. Seeing a group of African-American recruits from Louisiana stripped for a medical exam left a deep impression on one Union officer:

> Some of them were scarred from head to foot where they had been whipped. One man's back was nearly all one scar, as if the skin had been chopped up and left to heal

in ridges. Another had scars on the back of his neck, and from that all the way to his heels every little ways; but that was not such a sight as the one with the great solid mass of ridges from his shoulders to his hips. That beat all the antislavery sermons yet preached.[8]

At first, freedmen in the Western states were just as wary as the Sea Islanders had been of Union recruiters. Former field hands from plantations in the interior had not yet been exposed to Frederick Douglass's powerful arguments in favor of soldiering. "Liberty won by white men would lose half its value," he said. Douglass also thought blacks should be trained as a matter of course in the use of arms. "When it is once found that black men can give blows as well as take them, men will find more congenial employment than pounding them," he predicted.[9] Army agents, naturally, were skilled salesmen, and they could generally achieve their aims without resorting to force. Bounties, false promises, threats, and outrageous lies all were part of the recruiter's arsenal.

Mississippi refugees streamed into the Union camps, some fleeing the fighting, many bolting from hateful plantation labor, others simply exercising their newfound ability to move freely from one place to another. In November 1862, Grant assigned army chaplain John Eaton responsibility for "contrabands" in Union-occupied areas. Following Thomas Sherman's lead at Port Royal the year before, Grant ordered Eaton to put former slaves to work picking, ginning, and baling cotton. With Grant's approval, Eaton drew on army stores for tents, clothing, and rations. He also established a wage-labor system that forced Mississippi planters to pay former slaves if they wanted to keep operating.

The army employed blacks as laborers, though wage rates were low and payments often ran months behind. Government woodyards (yards that produced firewood for steamboats and stoves) hired many refugees; one yard in

Vicksburg eventually had more than 1,000 former slaves on the payroll collecting, chopping and stacking wood, though, again, wages barely reached subsistence level. Eaton's agents leased abandoned plantations to Northern businessmen and colluded to force blacks back to the cotton fields to work for low wages and in conditions so harsh they approached—sometimes exceeded—those of slavery. Though there were no rules barring African Americans from leasing plantation property, the majority lacked the money or credit to obtain land, supplies, and equipment for independent ventures. By one estimate, Mississippi blacks in 1864 held 7,000 acres out of a total of 100,000 acres of leased cottonlands.

One disaffected laborer had this to say about work and pay:

Former slaves responded enthusiastically to the new educational opportunities freedom made possible. Men, women, and children of all ages crowd into a Mississippi primary schoolroom in this wood engraving published in Harper's Weekly on June 23, 1866. (Library of Congress)

They said that we, the able-body men, was to get $8 a month, and the women, $4 and the ration; only we was to allow $1 the month to help the poor and then the old—which we don't regret—and one dollar for the sick ones, and then another dollar for *Gen'l Purposes*. We don't exactly know who that Gen'l is, but appears like there was a heap of them Gen'ls, and it takes all there is to pay 'em, 'cause we don't get nothing.[10]

Thousands of former slaves lived precariously in makeshift refugee camps. Badly built, with poor heating, light, and ventilation, the camps were breeding grounds for disease. Touring camps in Vicksburg and Natchez, Mississippi, in late 1863, Eaton found them overcrowded, unsanitary, and seriously mismanaged. People were "sickly, disheartened, dying on the streets," he reported, "not a family of them all either well-sheltered, clad or fed; no physicians, no medicines, no hospitals; many of the persons who had been charged with feeding them either sick or dead."[11]

Former slave John Roy Lynch, who would become a prominent politician in postwar Mississippi, managed through luck and his own sharp wits to escape the harshest consequences of the transition. He fled his Louisiana plantation a few weeks after the Union victory at Vicksburg, held down several jobs in succession, and somehow kept himself out of the refugee camps and the Union army.

Born in Concordia Parish, Louisiana, in 1847, the son of an enslaved mother and an Irish father, Lynch grew up as a favored house servant of the Alfred Davis family of Natchez. Mrs. Davis taught a Sunday-school class for slave children. One of her favorite lessons emphasized the distinction between a faithful servant and what she characterized as an "eye servant." An eye servant, Lynch recalled Mrs. Davis saying, "is one that will shirk his duty every chance he can get and will not work unless an eye is kept on him."[12] Young Lynch's duties involved opening and closing carriage doors for his mistress when she went out for a drive, and brushing flies away from the table during meals.

Bright, lively, and independent, he soon ran into trouble with Mrs. Davis, who had little tolerance for what she regarded as "sauciness." She banished Lynch to an outlying Davis plantation on the Louisiana side of the Mississippi River, with instructions that he be put to work in the fields. In the late summer of 1863, after word of Grant's military successes had drifted over to the Louisiana parishes, he ran away, crossed the river and slipped through the federal lines at Natchez. He had just turned 16 years old.

Lynch went to work as a waiter in a boardinghouse at $5 a month, then left that job to become a cook for the 49th Illinois. When the regiment moved six weeks later, Lynch tallied his earnings—a paltry $2. He finally found permanent work, at a living wage of $25 a month, as a pantryman aboard the river transport *Altamont*.

Ambitious and aggressive, Lynch kept moving up. Starting as a messenger at a photography studio, he soon learned enough about the trade to earn promotion to printer. Eventually, he took on the management of the shop for the absentee owner. Lynch also developed a keen appetite for knowledge. He attended a Yankee night school for four months, long enough to learn the rudiments of reading and writing. When pressure from Natchez whites forced the school to close, Lynch furthered his education by eavesdropping on recitations in the whites-only school across the alley.

"I could clearly and distinctly hear the questions and the responses," Lynch wrote in his autobiography. "In fact, I was sometimes so much absorbed that I would imagine, for the time being, that I was a member of the class and was eager to answer some of the questions."[13]

Like most blacks, Lynch clearly saw the importance of education in slavery's aftermath. Schools, land, the vote: these were the issues over which the great battles of Reconstruction would be fought. Meanwhile, Confederate resistance had to be crushed. Major General William T. Sherman's 285-mile March to the Sea in November–December 1864 advanced both causes immeasurably.

Sherman's forces swept eastward across Georgia, tearing up railroad tracks, setting fires, plundering without restraint. "One could track the line of Sherman's march by the fires on the horizon," a former Confederate officer told Northern traveler John T. Trowbridge a few weeks after the war's end. "He burned the gin-houses, cotton-presses, railroad depots, bridges, freight-houses, and unoccupied dwellings. He stripped our people of everything. He deserves to be called the Great Robber of the nineteenth century."[14]

Many African Americans, of course, saw Sherman as the great liberator. "They flock to me, old and young," the general wrote, "they pray and shout and mix up my name with Moses."[15] Thousands, perhaps as many as 25,000, left their home plantations to follow the Union army. Sherman tried to discourage the exodus. Knowing he could not provide food, clothing, or shelter, he urged the freed people to stay at home until the occupation forces arrived.

Still, the lure of emancipation proved irresistible. Union troops dealt ruthlessly with those who got in the way of the advance. With varying degrees of force, the Yankees simply pushed the refugees aside. An untold number perished along the route. "The waters of the Ogeechee and Ebenezer Creek can account for hundreds who were blocking up our columns, and there abandoned," a Union officer reported. "Many of them died in the bayous and lagoons of Georgia."[16] Even so, large groups of former slaves trailed Sherman's columns into Savannah, which Union forces occupied on December 21.

With the conclusion of the military operation, Sherman turned his attention to the refugee problem. At first, he proposed sending thousands of freed people north to Port Royal. But the commander there, Brigadier General Rufus Saxton, discouraged the notion. "Every cabin and house on

Freed people tend sweet potatoes, a staple food crop, on Hopkinson's Plantation, Edisto Island, S.C., in 1862. (Library of Congress)

these islands is filled to overflowing," he explained.[17] Then, in mid-January 1865, Sherman launched a first step toward a potentially revolutionary program of land redistribution.

Sherman's Special Field Orders No. 15 reserved the Georgia and South Carolina Sea Islands and the abandoned plantations along rivers for 30 miles inland for the freed people. Each family could obtain a 40-acre plot; Sherman also authorized the temporary loan of partially broken-down army horses and mules. The order hinted strongly that the government eventually would confirm individual titles to the plots.

Sherman claimed later that he never intended the land distribution to be permanent. Nevertheless, his program gave rise to the persistent postwar legend of "forty acres and a mule" that sprang up among the freed people. By June 1865, some 40,000 blacks had been settled on 400,000 acres of "Sherman land." As news of the distribution spread, freed people throughout the South came to believe that the government would give them a homestead and the means to make a start on an independent life.

The federal army soon moved on, advancing northward through the Carolinas and leaving a broad charred swath of destruction in its wake. General Saxton took charge of the land program. A Massachusetts native, the son of abolitionists, Saxton had a genuine commitment to the freed people. "He looks like a thoroughly *good* man," teacher Charlotte Forten remarked the first time she saw him.[18] Land ownership, Saxton believed, would guarantee a successful transition to freedom. He assured homesteaders they would receive clear titles to their 40 acres. He even dispensed sage agricultural advice, telling groups of black farmers to put as much as they could into the cash crops of cotton and rice. Saxton clearly expected the Sherman program to be a model for the postwar South.

By the summer of 1865, though, opposition to land reform had begun to build. Returning Confederates prepared to lay claim to their former property. They made allies of some Northerners with the argument that blacks working independently either would not or could not make a success of cotton growing. The freed people, they insisted, would not work without coercion. If the system of large, white-owned plantations were dismantled, there would be insufficient cotton to feed Northern mills.

Former slaves were contemptuous of such claims. "They have no reason to say we will not work, for we raised them, and sent them to school, and bought their land, and now it is as little as they can do to give us some of their land—be it little or much," asserted Union army veteran Melton R. Linton.[19] To Linton and many thousands of freed people,

The General and the Freedmen_____

War Secretary Edwin M. Stanton reached Savannah on January 9, 1865. General William T. Sherman, who had captured the city three weeks before, found the secretary curious about everything there, but especially about the freed people.

At Stanton's request, Sherman arranged for him to meet some 20 leaders of Savannah's black community. They were mostly ministers, and most had been born into slavery. One, an elderly Baptist preacher named Garrison Frazier, had been a slave for 60 years before managing to purchase his freedom in 1857.

The meeting took place in Sherman's rooms on January 12. The delegation elected Frazier to be spokesman, and Stanton and an aide put a series of questions to him.

How, Stanton wanted to know, did he define freedom?

"Freedom," answered Frazier, "is taking us from under the yoke of bondage and placing us where we could reap the fruit of our own labor."[23]

dividing the land among those who actually worked it seemed a matter of simple justice.

In October, the government issued direct orders barring further land allotments, and federal agents prepared to evict blacks who refused to make labor contracts to work for the returning owners. Saxton staunchly defended the homesteaders. "Could a just government drive out these loyal men?" he asked.[20] The answer, it soon became clear, was yes.

Former slaves strongly resisted returning to the old plantations as wage laborers. They continued to believe in the Sherman grants. "If I contract," one told John Trowbridge, "what good does my 40 acres do me?" Squatters on abandoned lands were equally confident. "General Saxton told me to come and stake out my 40 acres, and he'd give me a ticket," another freedman said.[21] This faith in the govern-

Did blacks prefer to live scattered among whites, or in their own communities?

"I would prefer to live by ourselves," said Frazier, speaking for himself, "for there is a prejudice against us in the South that will take years to get over."[24]

Sherman had been warned that Stanton had begun a whispering campaign against him in Washington, telling President Lincoln and others that he was hostile to the freed people, and especially toward the enlistment of blacks in the Union armies. Sherman may have been surprised when Stanton bluntly asked Frazier how blacks regarded the general. If so, the reply must have delighted him.

"We looked upon General Sherman as a man, in the providence of God, specially set apart to accomplish this work, and we unanimously felt inexpressible gratitude to him," Frazier said.[25]

Four days after the meeting, Sherman issued Special Field Orders No. 15, setting aside tens of thousands of acres of the low country for the exclusive homesteading of the freed people. ◆

ment proved to be sadly misplaced. In the end, Saxton could do nothing to help. In January 1866, Southern white political pressure forced his removal as the chief officer for freedmen's affairs on the southeast coast.

Events followed a similar course in the West. In Mississippi, the Treasury Department took over the plantation-leasing system from the army, which had badly mismanaged it. There were some reforms, some improvements: wages went up, and the government saw to it that payrolls were generally met, usually with half the agreed amount to be paid monthly, the balance due upon the sale of the crop.

Grant had authorized a Mississippi land reform experiment as early as 1863, confirming a settlement of freed people at Davis Bend below Vicksburg—the plantation lands of Joseph Davis and his brother, Confederate president Jefferson Davis. When Joseph Davis fled at the approach of Grant's army in 1862, his former slaves took over the management of the estate. Under the leadership of the entrepreneurial Benjamin Montgomery, the freed people were in firm control by the time the Union forces arrived.

In 1864, the government assigned the Davis land collectively to groups of African Americans; they paid only for army rations, tools, and draft animals. Nearly 5,000 men, women and children eventually settled at Davis Bend. The "colonists," as they called themselves, organized into companies to raise and market their crops. The Davis Bend farms raised 2,000 bales of cotton in 1865. At year's end, the company books showed a collective profit of nearly $160,000.

The government, however, did not choose to build on this unqualified success. In fact, Joseph Davis had all his holdings returned to him in January 1867. Freed people living and farming at Davis Bend were invited to stay on and work for Davis for wages.

But that is skipping ahead of the story. As commander in chief of all the Union land forces, Grant accepted the surrender of the main Confederate army in Virginia on April 9, 1865. Sherman's march through the Carolinas ended in the capitulation of a second rebel army. Confederates west of the Mississippi held out until the end of May. In those vast reaches, news of the federal triumph and emancipation traveled slowly. It was well into June before word of freedom reached Bexar County, Texas. Felix Haywood, a cowboy on a ranch near San Antonio, recalled how he and his fellow slaves reacted:

"Everybody went wild," Haywood said. "We all felt like horses and nobody had made us that way but ourselves. We was free. Just like that, we was free."[22]

NOTES

1. Leon F. Litwack, *Been in the Storm So Long: The Aftermath of Slavery* (New York: Alfred A. Knopf, 1979), 181.

2. Litwack, *Been in the Storm*, 215.

3. First quote, Kenneth M. Stampp, *The Era of Reconstruction, 1865–1877* (New York: Alfred A. Knopf, 1965), 123; second quote, Litwack, *Been in the Storm*, 119.

4. Litwack, *Been in the Storm*, 188.

5. Litwack, *Been in the Storm*, 213, 214, 224.

6. Litwack, *Been in the Storm*, 116.

7. Litwack, *Been in the Storm*, 123.

8. First quote, Bell I. Wiley, *The Life of Billy Yank: The Common Soldier of the Union* (Baton Rouge: Louisiana State University Press, 1990 reprint), 109; second quote, Wiley, *Billy Yank*, 115.

9. First quote, Herbert Aptheker, ed., *A Documentary History of the Negro in the United States*, Volume 1 (New York: Citadel Press, 1951), 478; second quote, Litwack, *Been in the Storm*, 75.

10. Litwack, *Been in the Storm*, 134.

11. Vernon L. Wharton, *The Negro in Mississippi, 1865–1900* (New York: Harper & Row, 1965), 42.

12. John Roy Lynch, *Reminiscences of an Active Life*, John Hope Franklin, ed. (Chicago: University of Chicago Press, 1970), 24.

13. Lynch, *Reminiscences*, 42–43.

14. John T. Trowbridge, *The South: A Tour of Its Battlefields and Ruined Cities* (New York: Arno Press, 1969 reprint), 475.

15. Eric Foner, *Reconstruction: America's Unfinished Revolution, 1863–1877* (New York: Harper & Row, 1988), 70.

16. Joel Williamson, *After Slavery: The Negro in South Carolina during Reconstruction, 1861–1877* (Chapel Hill: University of North Carolina Press, 1965), 24–25.

17. *Official Record of the War of the Rebellion*, Volume 44 (Washington: U.S. Government, 1899), 787.

18. Charlotte Forten, *The Journal of Charlotte Forten*, Ray A. Billington, ed. (New York: W. W. Norton, 1981), 142.

19. Litwack, *Been in the Storm*, 273.

20. Foner, *Reconstruction*, 159.

21. Trowbridge, *The South*, 543 (both).

22. Litwack, *Been in the Storm*, 217.

23. William T. Sherman, *Memoirs of General W. T. Sherman* (New York: Library of America, 1990), 725–26.

24. Sherman, *Memoirs*, 726.

25. Sherman, *Memoirs*, 727.

3

A Tour in the South:
1863–1865

Four years of war had left much of the South in ruins. Richmond, Atlanta, and other cities were devastated. The armies had campaigned over vast areas of Virginia, the Carolinas, Georgia, Tennessee, Alabama, Mississippi, and Louisiana, trampling everything in their path. Southern whites were a beaten, demoralized people. With the destruction of slavery, the planter class lost most of its wealth. Returning Confederate soldiers and government officials expected to be punished: to forfeit their property, to be denied political rights, perhaps to be prosecuted for treason. For the South's 4 million African Americans, the war's end meant the hope of a new and better life.

Land, education, a political voice: former slaves demanded and expected these basic benefits of a free society.

Northern journalists who toured the South in the spring and summer of 1865 sent back vivid descriptions of a desolate land. In many parts of the country, food and other necessities were in critically short supply. As an emergency measure, Union forces fed the hungry in many cities and towns. Still, to perceptive Northerners, it sometimes seemed that while everything had changed, really nothing had changed. Amid the ruins, whites instinctively sought to preserve the ancient social and racial patterns. In Richmond, the former Confederate capital, Connecticut journalist John Trowbridge noted in the summer of 1865, whites and blacks were not permitted to draw their "destitute rations" from the same place.

White and black, Southerners got along as best they could, scrabbling for a subsistence. Touring the crumbling, weed-grown fortifications near Petersburg, Virginia, where the Battle of Crater occurred in July 1864 and where hundreds of black Union troops had been slaughtered in a bungled assault, Trowbridge found bent and rusted bayonets, canteens, and fragments of shells littering the barren ground. Fresh graves were all around. "In the earthworks near by I saw a negro man and woman digging out bullets. It was hard work, but they made a living at it."[1] The couple told him they got four cents a pound for spent lead in Petersburg.

In some places, groups of African Americans managed to build thriving communities on top of the rubble. Retreating Confederates had set fire to Hampton, Virginia, leaving only a dozen or so buildings still standing. Refugee former slaves moved in. They put up split-board huts for shelter and cultivated small farms, none larger than 40 acres, on the outskirts of town. "The height of the freedmen's ambition was to have little homes of their own and to work for themselves," Trowbridge observed.[2] But he saw, too, that the former white owners were already beginning to return,

Contrabands—the Union army's term for escaped or newly freed slaves—at the Foller Farm, Cumberland Landing, Va., in 1862. For many former slaves, emancipation meant reunions of long-seperated family members. (Library of Congress)

scouting the ruined town and preparing to reclaim their property.

Another Northern journalist, Ohioan Whitelaw Reid, toured a freedmen's school in Hampton in the spring of 1865. He found more than 200 pupils at their desks, with the convalescent Union soldiers who served as teachers padding about in their hospital slippers. At first, it struck Reid as strange to see boys of 15 or 16 working in the First Reader. Then he saw how eagerly they plunged into the material. Everywhere he went, he remarked on the enthusiasm with which the older freed people—young men and women, the middle-aged, even the elderly—approached their lessons.

Illiteracy, it turned out, knew no racial bounds in Virginia in 1865. If few blacks could read, many whites were unlettered too—a full third of the population. "These whites don't read and write because they don't want to," one freedman thought. "Our people don't because the law and public feeling are against it. The ignorant white had every chance to learn, but didn't; we had every chance to remain ignorant, and many of us learned in spite of them."[3]

For many blacks, the ability to move about freely, to come and go "like bees trying to find a setting place," in one former slave's phrase, was the first tangible evidence of emancipation. Before the first schools opened, before the first 40-acre plots were distributed, there was mobility. Some ex-slaves went off in search of friends or relatives. Some were looking for work or food. Some were in motion simply because, for the first time in their lives, they could journey from one town to the next without risking a violent encounter with the slave patrol.

This restlessness confirmed the suspicions of many Southern whites that the freed people were interested mainly in avoiding work or in causing trouble. Union officer John De Forest had another view:

> They had a passion, not so much for wandering, as for getting together; and every mother's son among them seemed to be in search of his mother; every mother in search of her children. In their eyes the work of emancipation was incomplete until the families which had been dispersed by slavery were reunited.[4]

Former slaves tested this aspect of freedom again and again, as though they had trouble believing it could last. "The negroes don't seem to feel free unless they leave their old homes," a Florida planter wrote, "just to make sure they can go when and where they choose." One woman turned down an offer of high wages if she would stay on as a cook in the old household. "If I stay here I'll never know I'm free," she told her late mistress.[5] The woman only traveled as far as the next village—but she traveled.

Some of the most poignant documents of emancipation were the appeals to broken-up families that appeared regularly in Southern newspapers for many years after the war.

> Information wanted, of Caroline Dodson, who was sold from Nashville, Nov. 1st, 1862, by James Lumsden to Warwick (a trader in human beings), who carried her to Atlanta, Georgia, and she was last heard of in the sale pen of Robert Clarke (human trader in that place), from which she was sold. Any information of her whereabouts will be thankfully received and rewarded by her mother. Lucinda Lowery, Nashville.[6]

Union agents, missionaries, and teachers helped whenever they could, though few searchers were able to supply more than a kinsman's first name and perhaps the state where he had last been seen. Many a letter was thus addressed to "Joe" in Tennessee or "Ella" in North Carolina. A hopeful Mississippi freedman dictated this note to a brother in Virginia from whom he had been parted for more than 20 years:

> I'm going to buy a lot, and build me a hut on it; and then, Jack, you is wanted down here, to see your old brother. For the last time he saw you, he was standing on the auction block, and Mass'r Bill was turning him around, like a possum on the spit, so's the driver would see him fair and square. Never mind, Jack. I'm trying to let bygones go, and just look out for number one, and I'm powerful glad I'm a free man now. Come Christmas, if you can, Jack.[7]

Some enslaved people took to the road to escape harsh plantation conditions, especially in interior districts where white acceptance of emancipation came grudgingly. In remote corners of the South, Union authorities were distributing circulars informing blacks of the end of slavery well into the summer of 1865. Whitelaw Reid found a large number of refugees in Wilmington, North Carolina in May 1865. "They do not wish to trust their old masters on the plantations," he thought, "and without any definite purpose or plan, they have a blind but touching instinct, that wherever the flag is floating is a good place for friendless negroes to go."[8] In these unsettled times, any Yankee outpost offered a measure of security.

Beyond food, shelter, and movement, there were manners and social usages to be learned and unlearned, formalities to be observed. Few plantation slaves had surnames, especially among the field hands. After emancipation, there was a great rush to adopt last names. Many, of course, saluted the heroes of abolition with their choices. "They named their selves big names," a freedman remembered. "Some of the names was Abraham and some called their selves Lincoln. Any big name, except their master's name. It was the fashion."[9] Some, too, adopted the names of local officials who had been kind or helpful; one young man dubbed himself States Attorney Smith.

Sympathetic Yankees sometimes went out of their way to perform commonplace acts of courtesy, unheard of in slavery days, that emphasized the new state of affairs. A Virginia freedwoman named Eliza Sparks recalled a brief meeting with a Union officer who asked her the name of the child she was carrying on her hip.

"Charlie, like his father."

"Charlie what?"

"I told him Charlie Sparks."

The officer gave the baby a copper coin and took his leave with a "Good-bye, Mrs. Sparks."

"Now what you think of that," Eliza Sparks mused in telling the story many years later, still warmed by the recollection of the white officer's manner.[10]

Nothing did more to call attention to the new circumstances than the appearance of the black Union troops. Teacher Charlotte Forten told of one Sea Islander who delighted in the impotent rage with which "Secesh" reacted to the sight of armed blacks wearing the national uniform. For many freedmen in the ranks, a return to the former precincts of slavery could be emotionally overwhelming. From the old North Carolina seaport town of Wilmington, an ex-slave in Yankee uniform wrote:

> We march through these fine thoroughfares where once the slave was forbid being out after nine P.M., or to puff a 'regalia,' or to walk with a cane, or to ride in a carriage! Negro soldiers!—with banners floating.[11]

Tens of thousands of freedmen enlisted in the Union army. These soldiers were teamsters serving with the Army of the James at Bermuda Hundred, Virginia. (Library of Congress)

Most Southern whites accepted defeat, emancipation, and occupation with sullen, resentful silence, at least at first. In May and June 1865, Reid found the whites he encountered to be quietly submissive, "awaiting whatever course the victors might see fit to pursue."[12] That began to change, gradually, as Confederate soldiers returned home and as the attitude of Lincoln's successor in the White House, Andrew Johnson, became clearer. Johnson's liberal granting of pardons enabled former rebels to begin the process of reclaiming their property and to think of becoming involved in postwar public life.

Inland, where federal troops were spread thinnest, members of the planter class continued to exercise their traditional authority. Remarked Reid:

> The masters tell [the ex-slaves] that slavery is to be restored as soon as the army is removed; that the Government is already mustering the army out of service; that next year, when the State is re-organized, the State authorities will control slavery. Meantime, the negroes are worked as hard as ever—in some cases harder—and they have no more protection from the cruelty of whites than ever.[13]

Planter-class whites impoverished by the war wondered how they would survive. Who would get a cash crop into the ground? Who would tend the livestock? Who would prepare and serve the meals? "We have nothing left to begin new with," a South Carolina planter told John Trowbridge. "I never did a day's work in my life, and don't know how to begin." Soon enough, though, they accommodated themselves to emancipation. "The master says we are all free," a former slave in South Carolina said, "but it don't mean we are white. And it don't mean we are equal."[14] As the shock of defeat wore off, whites became increasingly aggressive in reasserting social control.

White Southerners brooded obsessively over matters of racial etiquette. A freedman's slightest lapse from an attitude of slave-era servility could provoke a diatribe. "Negroes neglected to touch their hats to overseers or masters whom they disliked; and straightaway it was announced that they were growing too saucy for human endurance," Reid wrote. "They refused to be beaten; and, behold, the grossest insubordination was existing among negroes." A Tennessee white entertained his fellow steamboat passengers with this story of black "impudence":

> Last week, in Chattanooga, I said to a nigger I found at the railroad, 'Here, Buck! Show me the baggage-room.' He said, 'My name a'n't Buck.' I just put my six-shooter to his head, and by _____! he didn't stop to think what his name was, but showed me what I wanted.[15]

In many localities, agents of the federal Freedmen's Bureau did what they could to protect former slaves from such acts of individual terrorism. Congress created the bureau in March 1865 to provide food, clothing, and medical care to freed slaves, to introduce a free labor system to the South, to establish schools, and to resolve conflicts between blacks and whites. The act also authorized the bureau to resettle African Americans on small plots of confiscated or abandoned land.

This was a tall order for an organization with no staff and no budget. "It is not in your power to fulfill one tenth of the expectations of those who framed the bureau," General Sherman wrote the first freedmen's commissioner, General Oliver Otis Howard. "I fear you have Hercules' task."[16] Howard had to draw on the War Department for agents, supplies, and funds, and to rely on Northern charitable organizations for further assistance to carry out an unprecedented campaign of social reform.

At its peak strength, the Freedmen's Bureau employed barely 900 agents, so redress in cases such as that of the

These prosperous-looking former slaves pose with a mule and cart in front of a newly built cabin on Edisto Island, S.C. Emancipation provided the first opportunities for black Southerners to own their own land. (New-York Historical Society)

former slave in Chattanooga was rare. In his memoir of Freedmen's Bureau service in South Carolina, agent John De Forest noted that he was responsible for an area of 3,000 square miles with a population of 80,000. After the summer of 1865, Union army garrisons were too small and too widely scattered to enforce the law and guarantee blacks' civil rights.

Nor could the bureau help the victims of white reprisal. "A freedman is now standing at my door, his tattered clothes bespattered by blood from his head caused by blows inflicted by a white man with a stick and we can do nothing for him," an Alabama bureau agent wrote. "Yet these people flee to us for protection as if we could give it."[17] As violence escalated against blacks, the majority of federal agents found themselves powerless to intervene.

Still, the bureau managed to accomplish a great deal in its short life. In the first 13 months after the war, it issued 13 million rations (one ration of cornmeal, flour, and sugar supported a person for a week)—two thirds of the total to former slaves, the balance to white refugees. The agency established schools and supervised the educational initiatives of private Northern groups. Freedmen's Bureau hospitals cared for the sick and indigent. Bureau courts mediated wage and contract disputes and—unlike Southern civilian courts—made an effort to approach the ideal of equality before the law for former slaves. There were few prosecutions for vagrancy or "insolence" in the Freedmen's Bureau judiciary.

Some African Americans mistrusted the bureau. Most agents were white. Some were unblushingly racist. Freedmen disliked being pressured into signing labor contracts and they resented white interference with developing black social, educational, and political institutions.

For many white Southerners, the Freedmen's Bureau and all its works were detestable. Agents often were seen as promoters of equality between the races. Yet the bureau frequently operated to the benefit of landowning whites. Following the army's wartime precedent in Port Royal, northern Mississippi, and elsewhere, bureau agents pressured the freed people to return to work as plantation wage laborers, discouraging their efforts to acquire their own land.

Native whites strenuously resisted black attempts to buy or even lease land. "The feeling is so strong," Reid said, "that the man who should sell small tracts to [blacks] would be in actual personal danger."[18] Under the contract system, freed people frequently complained of nonpayment of wages or unfair division of crops. In turn, whites complained that former slaves failed to hold up their end of the bargain and sought Freedmen's Bureau help in enforcing labor contracts.

In New Orleans, an Island of Freedom

The 11,000 free blacks of New Orleans formed the largest such community in the Deep South in the years before the Civil War. Many were Creoles—the literate, well-to-do descendants of French settlers and slave women. They practiced skilled crafts such as bricklaying, cigarmaking, and carpentry. There were free black architects, doctors, jewelers, musicians, and undertakers. A few were wealthy slaveholding planters. Sugar planter Antoine Dubuclet, for example, owned 100 slaves.

The free blacks of New Orleans generally were denied the vote, and there were many other social and political inequities. Unlike enslaved African Americans, however, they could own property, sue (and be sued), and travel more or less without restriction.

When Union forces occupied New Orleans in the spring of 1862, hundreds of free blacks came forward to volunteer to fight against the Confederacy. In August, the federal commander, Major General Benjamin Butler, authorized the raising of three black regiments, the First, Second and Third Louisiana Native Guards. By November, some 3,000 men had joined the colors and were serving under officers drawn from the free black community.

Reid told of a woman laborer who, after collecting her wages on quarterly payday, announced that she would be leaving to rejoin her husband on a distant plantation.

"Don't you know that you contracted with me for a year?" the plantation lessee, a Northerner, asked.

"Don't know nothin' about it. I want to go away."

"Haven't you been well treated here?"

"Yes."

"Well, I'm keeping my part of the contract, and you've got to keep yours. If you don't, I'll send you to jail, that's all."[19]

"Our great desire is to strike a Blow for the Union, therefore we are both willing and ready to forsake our wives and children and risk the fortunes of War," guardsman John B. Bernabe asserted.[27]

With emancipation, the free blacks of New Orleans campaigned on behalf of former slaves for the vote, for public schools, and for an end to discrimination in public places. They also formed aid societies for the freed people. One such agency, the Bureau of Industry, distributed emergency food and fuel assistance and helped freedmen find jobs.

Still, free blacks, the majority of whom were mulattoes (people of mixed ancestry), did not always recognize a community of interest with former slaves. Freedmen's Bureau agents reported, for example, that some free blacks were reluctant to send their children to freedmen's schools. Said one observer:

> They tended to separate their struggle from that of the Negroes. Some believed they would achieve their cause more quickly if they abandoned the black to his fate. In their eyes, they were nearer to the white man; they were more advanced than the slave in all respects.[28]

Many free blacks evidently hoped to occupy a privileged middle ground between the dominant white community and the emergent community of former slaves. But in fact, both groups of African Americans, the historically free and the newly free, had everything to gain should the experiment of Reconstruction succeed. ◆

Still, some former slaves learned the hard way what a contract could mean. "I put my finger to pencil to sign a contract to work all summer for one tenth of the crop, and when it was harvested, I had one quart of molasses and one bushel of corn, and I and my family were sent away," a South Carolina freedwoman reported.[20]

Planters resented the fact that many blacks refused to work the long hours, from early dawn to evening twilight, that had been customary during slavery. Mississippi Freedmen's Bureau agent Samuel Thomas soon grew tired of hearing the planters' litany about black idleness.

It is nonsense to talk so much about getting the negroes to work. Who are the workmen in these fields? Who are hauling the cotton to market, driving hacks and drays in the cities, repairing streets and railroads, cutting timber, and in every place raising the hum of industry? The freedmen, not the rebel soldiery. There are today as many idle white men as there are negroes in the same condition, yet no arrangements are made for their working.[21]

Conscientious Freedmen's Bureau agents made efforts to persuade landowners to deal honestly with their laborers. When Georgia whites complained of the unwillingness of blacks to sign on as field workers, bureau agent John E. Bryant offered what sounded like a reasonable rejoinder. "Let it be understood that a fair day's wages will be paid for a fair day's work," he said, "and the planter will not want for reliable and faithful laborers." A Galveston, Texas newspaper editor who generally sympathized with white landowners saw to the heart of the problem. "There are men who truly complain that they cannot get field hands," he wrote. "But they are men of known brutality or financial weakness."[22] In the end, when it became clear that the federal government would offer no large-scale homesteading program for former slaves, the great majority had no choice but to return to plantation labor. And most did so.

Along with land, the freed people sought a share of political power. In the early phases of Reconstruction, Union political transactions were restricted to whites. During the war, President Lincoln had outlined a program by which the Union-occupied states of Louisiana, Arkansas, and Tennessee were partially reconstructed. Under Lincoln's lenient program, citizens could organize a state government when 10 percent of the voters had taken a loyalty oath.

The collapse of slavery had come quickly in New Orleans and the Louisiana sugar parishes. Some planters tried to preserve vestiges of the institution, though with scant success. "If you think slavery exists, go out in the streets and see if you can get your slave to obey you," one skeptical white said.[23] Conceding the point, Unionist Louisiana whites adopted a revised constitution in 1864 that acknowledged the end of slavery.

Still, Unionists in the three states made no provisions for African-American political involvement. Lincoln had said nothing about granting the vote to former slaves. (Blacks, it should be remembered, were denied the vote in most Northern states before 1865.) The president apparently intended to leave the question of black suffrage up to the states. In consequence, the first reconstructed states limited the franchise to whites. There is evidence that Lincoln had given at least some consideration to a measure of black suffrage. There were, for example, several thousand freeborn persons of color in New Orleans. Many were well-educated and prosperous; some had served in the Union army. In March 1864, the president accepted a suffrage petition from two representatives of this long-established free community. A day or so later, Lincoln wrote to a prominent Louisiana Unionist about the possibility of granting the vote to freeborn African Americans. "But this is only a suggestion," the president added; and nothing came of it.[24] The effect of Lincoln's caution was to deny blacks a political voice in wartime Louisiana, Arkansas, and Tennessee.

Conservatives advanced all the familiar arguments against black suffrage: former slaves were too ignorant to vote; they were incapable of self-government. That, of course, begged the question of low levels of white education in much of the South. "My freedmen are far more intelligent and better prepared to vote than the white population around us," a Maury County, Tennessee politician told John Trowbridge.[25] Besides, the freedmen were loyal to the Union. In Louisiana in 1864, General Nathaniel P. Banks, the Union commander, permitted former Confederates who had taken the loyalty oath to vote, while all African Americans were excluded.

Even so, few of the freed people abandoned their faith in a brighter future, even in the face of numerous setbacks and defeats. In New Orleans in June 1865, Reid found a white-haired old man, 60 or so, in a schoolroom full of children ages 4 to 14. Like the others, he was working in the First Reader. "He believed," remarked Reid, "that as soon as he could read, he would be entitled to vote."[26]

NOTES

1. John T. Trowbridge, *The South: A Tour of Its Battlefields and Ruined Cities* (New York: Arno Press, 1969 reprint), 211.

2. Trowbridge, *The South*, 222.

3. Whitelaw Reid, *After the War: A Tour of the Southern States, 1865–1866*, C. Vann Woodward, ed. (New York: Harper & Row, 1965), 145.

4. John De Forest, *A Union Officer in the Reconstruction*, James H. Crushore and David M. Potter, eds. (New Haven: Yale University Press, 1948), 36.

5. Leon F. Litwack, *Been in the Storm So Long: The Aftermath of Slavery* (New York: Alfred A. Knopf, 1979), 297.

6. Litwack, *Been in the Storm*, 232.

7. Litwack, *Been in the Storm*, 232.

8. Reid, *After the War*, 50.

9. Litwack, *Been in the Storm*, 249.

10. Litwack, *Been in the Storm*, 121.

11. Litwack, *Been in the Storm*, 95.

12. Reid, *After the War*, 136.

13. Reid, *After the War*, 51.

14. First quote, Trowbridge, *The South*, 291; second quote, Litwack, *Been in the Storm*, 224.

15. First quote, Reid, *After the War*, 386–87; second quote, Trowbridge, *The South*, 238–39.

16. Eric Foner, *Reconstruction: America's Unfinished Revolution, 1863–1877* (New York: Harper & Row, 1988), 143.

17. Foner, *Reconstruction*, 148.

18. Reid, *After the War*, 564.

19. Reid, *After the War*, 530.

20. Mary Ames, *A New England Woman's Diary in Dixie* (New York: Negro Universities Press, 1969 reprint), 120.

21. Vernon L. Wharton, *The Negro in Mississippi, 1865–1900* (New York: Harper & Row, 1965), 80.

22. First quote, Foner, *Reconstruction*, 155; second quote, Rembert W. Patrick, *Reconstruction of the Nation* (New York: Oxford University Press, 1967), 39.

23. Foner, *Reconstruction*, 49.

24. Foner, *Reconstruction*, 49.

25. Trowbridge, *The South*, 282.

26. Reid, *After the War*, 253.

27. John W. Blassingame, *Black New Orleans, 1860–1880* (Chicago: University of Chicago Press, 1973), 35.

28. Foner, *Reconstruction*, 48.

4

Race, Caste, and Class: 1865

The freed people moved
quickly to set up independent institutions and put their own
imprint on schools and other organizations under Northern
sponsorship. In many communities an African-American
leadership, often drawn from a pool of preachers, schoolteachers, and ex-soldiers, began to emerge. The legal system
and questions of land ownership and tenure were the chief
concerns of former slaves in the immediate aftermath of
emancipation. Education was their chief opportunity.

Blacks were as insistent about achieving equality before
the law as about any other single issue. They sought the right
to testify in court and to serve on juries. Southern whites
fought fiercely to deny them these basic civil rights. Blacks

also campaigned for multiracial police forces. "The police of this place make the law to suit themselves," a black schoolteacher in Alabama charged—a state of affairs that prevailed in most places in the South in the absence of federal supervision.[1]

Where it operated unchecked during the summer and autumn of 1865, Southern white justice proved to be something worse than a farce. When a Northern journalist inquired about the crimes of a group of black men sentenced to a Selma, Alabama chain gang, he discovered that the most serious infractions involved blacks' use of abusive language to whites. "It was a singular fact that no white men were ever sentenced to the chain gang—being, I suppose, all virtuous," the journalist observed.[2] In the Southern system of separate and unequal justice, courtrooms were sometimes equipped with two Bibles to swear on, one for whites, the other for blacks.

Conversely, whites escaped serious punishment for even the most severe crimes against African Americans. In an extreme case, an Ocala, Florida court tried a white man for the murder of a black, found him guilty, and sentenced him to a $225 fine and one minute in jail. In a more representative instance, a New Orleans white spent a day in jail for stealing a pair of shoes worth $13. On the same day, in the same court, a black thief received a three-month jail term for taking shirts and petticoats valued at $18.

Whenever possible, the freed people turned to fellow African Americans for assistance or advice. Blacks who had lived in the free states for a long time and had been educated there were a natural source of leadership. Aaron Bradley, born enslaved in South Carolina, escaped in the 1830s, made his way north, and studied law in Boston. He returned to the Georgia–South Carolina low country in 1865 to counsel former slaves on questions of land ownership. Another black, Martin Delany, helped recruit black soldiers during the war and served as a Freedmen's Bureau agent in the Port Royal area from 1865 to 1868. Francis L. Cardozo, a

Robert Smalls, shown here in a photograph taken after 1875, became a hero in the North after his daring escape in the Confederate steamer Planter. *He represented the South Carolina low country in the U.S. Congress.* (Library of Congress)

Congregational minister, returned to his native South Carolina a few weeks after the war ended to become principal of the Morris Street School in Charleston. He also played a key role in establishing teacher training programs for blacks.

A native leadership developed as well. Robert Smalls, born enslaved in Beaufort, South Carolina, became perhaps the best-known African-American war hero for his exploit of sailing the steamer *Planter*, with its crew of slaves, out of Charleston Harbor under the Confederate guns in 1862. "I thought the *Planter* might be of use to Uncle Abe," Smalls explained.[3] Returning to Beaufort after the war, Smalls became a successful merchant, and, for many years, the unchallenged political chief of the Sea Islands. Army veteran Prince Rivers, another former slave, served as a legislator and trial justice in upcountry South Carolina. Mississippian John Lynch, whose former mistress had banished him to the cotton fields for showing his independence, entered politics as a justice of the peace and won election to the state legislature and, later, to Congress.

Regardless of their background or attitude, black leaders were in consensus on the priority of education as a means of advancement. Increasing white resistance to blacks' efforts to use the schools to forward their aims only confirmed the leaders' resolve. "Our weapons are the spelling book, the Bible, the press and the implements of industry; our impregnable fortifications are schoolhouses and the church," ex-slave Henry H. Garnett declared.[4] Hundreds of schools were established; thousands of former slaves learned the liberating value of literacy.

At first, most of the teachers in the freedmen's schools were Northerners. Altogether, some 5,000 Yankee volunteers taught in the South. They viewed their task, above all, as one of preparing former slaves for citizenship. For many, the most shocking and unforgiveable aspect of the old system was the ignorance in which masters had kept their slaves. A *New York Herald* correspondent took note of the confusion in one

Laura M. Towne poses with pupils in 1866. One of the orginal Gideonite volunteers, she taught in the South Carolina Sea Islands until her death in 1901. (New York Public Library, Photographs and Prints Division, Schomburg Center for Research in Black Culture)

black community about an upcoming election. "Quite a few thought it was the distribution of confiscated lands under a new name," he remarked. Charlotte Forten, the freeborn African-American teacher, asked the children in one of her classes what their ears were for. "One bright-eyed little girl answered promptly 'To put rings in,'" Forten recalled.[5] Bostonian Mary Ames, who came to Edisto Island, South Carolina to work with the Gideonites in May 1865, asked one of her pupils his age. A large child approaching adolescence, he told her he was three months old.

Classes were large, schoolhouses primitive, and books and other supplies scarce. Northern charitable organizations paid the teachers' modest salaries. Northern publishers sent 200,000 textbooks south. *The Freedmen's Book*, by New England reformer and abolitionist Lydia Maria Child, represents perhaps the best of the Northern effort. A collection of uplifting essays, poems and stories, household hints, and biographical sketches of prominent blacks, the book was used as an advanced text, often for adults, in the freedmen's schools. Child herself donated thousands of copies to the cause.

Child's simple, often elegantly phrased homilies were designed to gently instruct the freed people in the solid Yankee virtues of thrift, cleanliness, honesty, and the kind treatment of animals. A sample:

> Lashing a horse with a whip, to compel him to draw loads too heavy for his strength, makes him angry and discouraged; and at last, in despair of getting any help for his wrongs, he stands stock still when he finds himself fastened to a heavy load, and no amount of kicking or beating will make him stir. He has apparently come to the conclusion that it is better to be killed at once than to die daily. Slaves, who are under cruel task masters, also sometimes sink down in utter discouragement, and do not seem to care for being whipped to

death. The best way to cure the obstinate or disheartened laborer is to give him just wages and kind treatment; and the best way to deal with the discouraged and stubborn horse is to give him light loads and humane usage.[6]

Often, though, teachers found that few of their pupils were ready to use the comparatively sophisticated *Freedmen's Book*. Mary Ames and her friend Emily Bliss taught the ABCs, the days of the week, and counting to classes of as many as 140 former slaves of all ages. Young or old, Ames found the great majority of her students eager to learn. "Mighty anxious to know something," an old woman, bent with rheumatism, announced before her first session of evening school. One mid-June day, the Yankee teachers stayed at home, deciding it was too hot to walk the mile or so to the schoolhouse. After a while, the students came for the teachers. "We kept them and had school on the piazza," Mary Ames reported.[7]

Black ministers encouraged their congregations to establish formal societies for the purpose of raising money to build schools and pay teachers. Preachers often doubled as schoolmasters themselves, using the Bible as their primary text. Indeed, the desire for religious instruction brought many grown people into the classroom. In her diary, Ames wrote:

> A woman came with a prayer-book, asking to be taught to read it. We told her we would teach her willingly, but it would be some time before she could read. She was satisfied, and as she was leaving, put her hand under her apron and brought out two eggs—one she put in Emily's lap, the other in mine.[8]

Like many Northerners, Ames was struck by blacks' stubborn attachment to the small plots of land they had taken over, which they regarded as their own property. She too considered the Sherman land program to be a permanent feature of emancipation. "They have planted corn, beans, and cotton," she said of the people living on Edisto Island, South Carolina in May 1865, "and are to repay the Government when their crops are gathered."[9] Ames thought everyone—Yankee, Sea Islander, and returning planter alike—understood this circumstance.

Also understood, she and others believed, was the notion that the government eventually would validate freed people's titles to the abandoned lands. When planter Stephen Elliot returned to Beaufort after the Confederate collapse, his former slaves greeted him with pleasure. "They were delighted to see me, and treated me with overflowing affection," he wrote. "They waited on me as before, gave me beautiful breakfasts and splendid dinners [but] they firmly and respectfully informed me: 'We own this land now. Put it out of your head that it will ever be yours again.'"[10] As abolitionist Thomas Wentworth Higginson noted, former slaves were not resentful of individuals so much as of the idea of planter ownership.

Planter Richard Fuller returned to the Sea Islands to find that his estate had been subdivided among former slaves. One-time field hand Jim Cashman greeted his former master with an offer to show him around the neighborhood:

> The Lord has blessed us since you have been gone. It used to be Mr. Fuller No. 1, now it is Jim Cashman No. 1. Would you like to take a drive through the island, Sir? I have a horse and buggy of my own now, Sir, and I would like to take you to see my own little lot of land and my new house on it, and I have as fine a crop of cotton, Sir, as ever you did see, if you please—and Jim can let you have ten dollars if you want them, Sir.[11]

Still, the Sea Islanders had reckoned without Abraham Lincoln's successor. Though few knew much about Andrew

Johnson's politics, many blacks seemed instinctively to understand that they had lost a potential ally with Lincoln's murder in April 1865. "Uncle Sam is dead, isn't he?" the Port Royal missionaries were asked. "The government is dead, isn't it? You have got to go North and Secesh come back, haven't you? We going to be slaves again?"[12] In fact, Johnson began almost at once to take steps that would return the prewar planter class to power.

Born into poverty in North Carolina, Andrew Johnson had no formal schooling when he opened a tailor shop in Greenville, Tennessee in 1826. His wife taught him to write. He launched a political career as the scourge of the planter aristocracy—"a cheap purse-proud set they are," Johnson thought, "not half as good as the man who earns his bread by the sweat of his brow." Not that he objected to slavery; he simply resented the fact that only the well-to-do could afford slaves. "I wish to God every head of a family in the United States had one slave to take the drudgery and menial service off his family," Johnson once said.[13] A former Democrat, as a Republican he became Lincoln's running mate in 1864 on a national union ticket.

In May 1865, with Congress in recess, this accidental president launched his program for the political reconstruction of the defeated South. At the same time, he offered amnesty for most rebels in return for a simple loyalty oath. Johnson appointed a provisional governor for each state, with authority to call a state convention and supervise the election of delegates. The convention would set voting and officeholding requirements. The voters would then choose a governor, a state legislature, and members of Congress. Each state would repudiate secession and would ratify the Thirteenth Amendment abolishing slavery. That accomplished, Johnson would revoke martial law and withdraw federal occupation forces.

State by state, the white South complied with Johnson's program. By December 1865, the president felt ready to declare the reconstruction process complete. In nearly every state, the planter class had regained power. In an extreme case, former Confederate vice president Alexander Stephens of Georgia won election to the U.S. Senate. The Johnson governments, as they were known, made no effort to grant even limited political rights to blacks. Some states expressly barred persons of color from voting. "Ours is, and it ever shall be, a government of white men," Mississippi governor Benjamin G. Humphries, an ex-Confederate brigadier, announced at his inaugural.[14] One by one, the Johnson legislatures adopted the so-called Black Codes—restrictive laws applying only to blacks that were nearly as severe as those of slavery times.

National black leaders protested the repressive new Southern state governments all the way to the White House. Frederick Douglass, America's leading black abolitionist, headed a delegation that met with President Johnson early in 1866. "We are not satisfied with an amendment prohibiting slavery," one of the delegates, George Downing, told the president. "We wish it enforced with appropriate legislation. We ask for it intelligently, with the knowledge and conviction that the fathers of the Revolution intended freedom for every American; that they should be protected in their rights as citizens and be equal before the law."

Johnson replied that he would not risk a race war by forcing black rights on a hostile white South.

"You enfranchise your enemies and disenfranchise your friends," Douglass responded. But that was as far as the discussion went. Johnson remained firmly opposed to a black role in public life.[15]

Restoration of the old order emboldened whites and discouraged the freed people. On St. Helena Island, South Carolina, teacher Laura Towne had an explanation for some blacks' shows of affection for the returning planters. "The people receive the rebels better than we expected," she wrote, "but the reason is they believe Johnson is going to put them in their old masters' hands again, and they feel they must conciliate or be crushed."[16] Their fears proved all too justified. As early as the summer of 1865, the president sent General Howard, the Freedmen's Bureau commissioner, to the low country to begin proceedings to evict blacks from abandoned lands.

Homesteaders on the "Sherman lands" would not leave quietly. In Georgia, Aaron Bradley, the Boston-trained African-American lawyer, urged resistance to the eviction orders. He was arrested and the removals were carried out. In South Carolina, black groups closely followed the debate over land questions in the Republican newspapers. Some 3,000 freed people turned out at a black church on Edisto Island to hear General Howard explain the government's change of policy and to encourage a return to the old plantations. "Why, General Howard," they asked, "do you take our lands away from us?" Many swore they would never again work for the "Secesh." According to Mary Ames, one man described his feelings this way: "He had lived all his life with a basket over his head," she reported, paraphrasing, "and now that it had been taken off and air and sunlight had come to him, he could not consent to have the basket over him again."[17]

The Gideonites were sympathetic but powerless. "The white people of Edisto Island have indeed suffered," Ames wrote, "but now their homes are to be given back to them. The island negroes and those brought here by our bewildered, blundering government have, and will have, harder days than the masters." After delivering the bitter news, Howard appointed a three-member freedmen's committee to consider the fairest way of restoring the planters' lands. The general, who had lost an arm in the fighting on the Virginia Peninsula in 1862, asked the freedmen to forgive those who had enslaved them, just as he had forgiven his wartime enemy. The committee responded:

You ask us to forgive the owners of our island. *You* only lost your right arm in the war and might forgive them. The man who tied me to a tree and gave me 39 lashes and who stripped and flogged my mother and my sister and who will not let me stay in his empty hut except I will do his planting and be satisfied with his price and who combines with others to keep away land from me well knowing I would not have anything to do with him if I had land of my own—that man, I cannot well forgive. Does it look as if he has forgiven me, seeing how he tries to keep me in a condition of helplessness?[18]

Mary Ames noticed, now, that sometimes a freedman would reject a returning planter's 'Howdy' and outstretched hand. Rejected, too, were the standard New Year's offers of labor contracts. The Yankee soldiers made the rounds of the islands with the government's eviction notices. "In February," Ames wrote, "we saw all the negroes coming in from the fields, their hoes over their shoulders. They told us that the guard had ordered them to leave the plantation if they would not work for the owners. Sorely troubled they appealed to us. We could only tell them to obey orders."[19]

The Port Royal experiment had been carried out in a blaze of publicity. The big Northern newspapers had sent back detailed progress reports. Northern volunteers had powerful allies in reform circles at home, and there was a continuing presence of strong federal authority. Thus, blacks in the South Carolina low country had protections that were not generally available elsewhere. In much of the South, reaction to emancipation had been savage. Few whites could imagine the freed people in any other role than as laborers in the cotton and rice fields. "The negroes are no more free than they were forty years ago," Tennessee politician Emerson Etheridge declared, "and if anyone goes about the country telling them they are free, shoot him."[20] A Georgia planter told a Northern observer quite seriously that he deemed one

A Half-Finished Revolution _____

At President Johnson's request, former Union general Carl Schurz set out on a fact-finding tour of the South in July 1865. An amateur soldier but a professional politician and journalist, Schurz maintained close ties to the Radical Republicans in Congress, strong supporters of civil and political rights for former slaves. German-born, a student leader in the 1848 revolution who had fled Germany after the collapse of the democratic movements there, his attitude toward the freed people was sympathetic.

Schurz found a South that had not yet accepted the reality of emancipation. "The negro exists for the special object of raising cotton, rice and sugar *for the whites*," he wrote, and Southerners believed "it is illegitimate for him to indulge, like other people, in the pursuit of his own happiness in his own way."[27] Given such attitudes, he thought, former slaves would need federal protection and assistance for years to come.

In his report to President Johnson, Schurz made a strong case for black suffrage. He had a simple answer to the argument that blacks were too

of his former slaves utterly unfit for freedom because the man had refused to submit to a whipping.

Some Southern whites seemed to recognize no bounds. After all, President Johnson's policy encouraged the view that the old relationships were to be largely restored. Whites had a "blind, baffled, vengeful hatred" of the freed people, journalist Whitelaw Reid thought. Their responses ranged from the ridiculous to the barbaric. Freedmen's Bureau agent John De Forest remarked on the absurd provisions many planters included in their labor contracts:

> [They] seemed to be unable to understand that work could be other than a form of slavery. Negroes must be respectful and polite; if they were not respectful and

ignorant to vote. "Practical liberty," he wrote, "makes a good school."[28] He also called for a broad program of land distribution so the freed people could be truly independent of the planter class.

In an appendix to the report, Schurz provided accounts documenting violence against blacks. It is a sickening catalog of racial crime: a woman scalped; a man whose beard and chin were cut off; a young girl beaten to death with a club; murders, rapes, and arsons innumerable.

The abolitionist leader Wendell Phillips once remarked that the Emancipation Proclamation freed slaves but ignored blacks. Acknowledging this, Schurz urged Johnson to implement an active federal program to fulfill the promise of freedom. "Nothing renders society more restless than a social revolution but half accomplished," he advised.[29]

When Schurz returned from his tour in September, the president evaded him. Johnson instead accepted a short memo from General Ulysses S. Grant based on a week-long excursion to a few Southern cities. Grant acknowledged that small federal garrisons would be necessary in the South, but he recommended sending only white troops, to avoid antagonizing former Confederates. ◆

polite they must pay a fine for each offense; they must admit no one on their premises unless by consent of the landowner; they must have a quiet household and not keep too many dogs; they must not go off the plantation without leave. The idea seemed to be that if the laborer were not bound body and soul he would be of no use.[21]

Attacks on freed people reached epidemic proportions. "The fact is," a North Carolina Freedmen's Bureau agent observed, "it's the first notion with a great many of these people, if a Negro says anything or does anything that they don't like, to take a gun and put a bullet into him."[22] Union ex-general Carl Schurz, who toured the South in the summer of 1865, collected evidence of countless acts of violence against blacks: shootings, hangings, arson attacks on schools and churches. Schurz strongly recommended against withdrawing U.S. forces from the South. Johnson refused to receive his report.

In later years, former slave Douglass Wilson, a Union army veteran, recalled how it had been when he and his neighbors sent their children off to school in New Orleans:

> We had no idea that we should see them return home alive in the evening. Big white boys and half-grown men used to pelt them with stones and run them down with open knives, both to and from school. Sometimes they came home bruised, stabbed, beaten half to death, and sometimes quite dead. My own son himself was often thus beaten. He has on his forehead to-day a scar over his right eye which sadly tells the story in those days of his efforts to get an education. I was wounded in the war, trying to get my freedom, and he over the eye, trying to get an education.[23]

Mississippi became the first state to adopt the detestable Black Codes. Under these laws, any ordinary white could arrest a black who violated a labor contract. Black people who could not prove they had work could be jailed. Blacks younger than 18 could be bound to an apprenticeship—to their former masters whenever possible. Blacks were barred from owning arms of any kind. They could not preach the gospel or sell liquor without a special license. They were forbidden to own or even rent land. Racial intermarriage was punishable by life imprisonment.

Other states followed Mississippi's lead. The codes set strict color-line restrictions for churches, schools, restaurants and hotels, public parks, and public conveyances such as streetcars, railroads, and steamboats. In South Carolina, blacks needed a license for any employment other than farm labor. Louisiana blacks could not leave their workplaces—usually plantations—without permission. In some states, Freedmen's Bureau commissioners issued orders repealing the more extreme provisions of the codes. Local authorities ignored the repeals, and bureau agents were powerless to enforce them anyway.

Here, then, was the system that presidential reconstruction set in place. Even some former slaveholders were appalled by the nearly complete abdication of federal authority. "To leave the negro to be dealt with by those whose prejudices are of the most bitter character against him will be barbarous," Mississippi planter R. W. Flournoy predicted.[24] His forecast proved only too accurate. White mobs, white secret societies such as the Ku Klux Klan, white police and court systems—all these in concert made freedom a precarious, often dangerous, condition for tens of thousands of African Americans.

The violence of the white reaction had begun to wear down the Northern volunteers. "I fear [support for black schools] can't be sustained after the novelty is over," Edward Philbrick wrote from Port Royal in the autumn of 1865. "There seems to be a lethargy creeping over our community . . . which is very hard to shake off." Some had simply tired of the former slaves' troubles. "Life among [the freed people] is a fearful thing for one's rose-colored ideas," Reid remarked.[25] Perceptive Northerners called this mix of disillusionment and weariness the "plantation bitters."

By year's end, the abandonment of the emancipated people seemed to have become an established fact. Gideonites Laura Towne and Cornelia Hancock returned utterly discouraged from a January 1866 meeting in Washington with President Johnson and War Secretary Stanton. "I know now how they stand," Hancock wrote. "The President has the power but not the will to do for the colored people. Stanton has the will and not the power to help."[26] Still, all was not lost. Johnson's stubbornness and continuing Southern white excesses were soon to drive Congress to launch what looked, for a brief historical moment, very much like a genuine attempt to build a just multiracial society on the ruins of the Confederacy.

NOTES

1. Leon F. Litwack, *Been in the Storm So Long: The Aftermath of Slavery* (New York: Alfred A. Knopf, 1979), 288.

2. John T. Trowbridge, *The South: A Tour of Its Battlefields and Ruined Cities* (New York: Arno Press, 1969 reprint), 435–36.

3. W. E. B. DuBois, *Black Reconstruction in America* (New York: Russell & Russell, 1962), 105.

4. Richard W. Murphy, *The Nation Reunited: War's Aftermath* (Alexandria, Va.: Time-Life Books, 1987), 42.

5. First quote, Murphy, *Nation Reunited*, 67; second quote, Charlotte Forten, *The Journal of Charlotte Forten*, Ray A. Billington, ed. (New York: W. W. Norton, 1981), 218.

6. Lydia Maria Child, *The Freedmen's Book* (New York: Arno Press, 1968 reprint), 98.

7. Both quotes, Mary Ames, *A New England Woman's Diary in Dixie* (New York: Negro Universities Press, 1969 reprint), 33, 59.

8. Ames, *New England Woman's Diary*, 31.

9. Ames, *New England Woman's Diary*, 17.

10. Willie Lee Rose, *Rehearsal for Reconstruction: The Port Royal Experiment* (Indianapolis: Bobbs, Merrill, 1964), 347–48.

11. Litwack, *Been in the Storm*, 202.

12. Elizabeth Ware Pearson, ed., *Letters from Port Royal, 1862–1868* (New York: Arno Press, 1969 reprint edition), 310–11.

13. Kenneth M. Stampp, *The Era of Reconstruction, 1865–1877* (New York: Alfred A. Knopf, 1965), 55, 56.

14. Stampp, *The Era of Reconstruction*, 78.

15. Leslie H. Fishel, Jr. and Benjamin Quarles, *The Black American: A Documentary History* (New York: William Morrow & Company, 1970), 275, 279.

16.   Laura M. Towne, *The Letters and Diary of Laura M. Towne*, Rupert M. Holland, ed. (New York: Negro Universities Press, 1969 reprint), 167.

17.   First quote, Eric Foner, *Reconstruction: America's Unfinished Revolution, 1863–1877* (New York: Harper & Row, 1988), 160; second quote, Ames, *New England Woman's Diary*, 98.

18.   First quote, Ames, *New England Woman's Diary*, 118; second quote, Foner, *Reconstruction*, 160.

19.   Ames, *New England Woman's Diary*, 122.

20.   Murphy, *Nation Reunited*, 29.

21.   First quote, Whitelaw Reid, *After the War: A Tour of the Southern States, 1865–1866*, C. Vann Woodward, ed. (New York: Harper & Row, 1965), 417; second quote, John De Forest, *A Union Officer in the Reconstruction*, James H. Crushore and David M. Potter, eds. (New Haven: Yale University Press, 1948), 28.

22.   Litwack, *Been in the Storm*, 277.

23.   Litwack, *Been in the Storm*, 279.

24.   Stampp, *The Era of Reconstruction*, 75.

25.   First quote, Pearson, ed., *Letters from Port Royal*, 317–18; second quote, Reid, *After the War*, xix.

26.   Rose, *Rehearsal for Reconstruction*, 356.

27.   Carl Schurz, *Report on the Condition of the South* (New York: Arno Press, 1969 reprint), 21.

28.   Schurz, *Report*, 43.

29.   Schurz, *Report*, 37.

5

The Radical Response:
1865–1868

With a simple expedient, congressional Republicans rejected President Johnson's reconstruction plan. When the 39th Congress convened in December 1865, the Republican majority refused to seat the newly elected Southern representatives and senators. The delegation included the former Confederate vice president, four former Confederate generals, and other high ex-officials of the Confederate government—"aggregations of white-washed rebels," Representative Thaddeus Stevens, the Radical Republican from Pennsylvania, called them.[1]

The president, it became clear, had made a turnabout. "Treason must be made odious and traitors must be punished and impoverished," Johnson had said a year or so before.[2]

Now, many senior rebels had been elected who were supposed to be ineligible for political office, even under the president's lenient amnesty program. Johnson skirted the issue by handing out wholesale pardons—a total of 13,500 were granted to former high-ranking Confederate military and civil officials by September 1867.

For many in Congress, the election results, coupled with the imposition of repressive Black Codes and continued violence against African Americans, only confirmed suspicions that white Southerners could not be trusted. Historian W. E. B. DuBois, writing in the 1930s, summed up conditions this way:

> There were four million freedmen and most of them on the same plantation, doing the same work that they did before emancipation. Moreover, they were getting about the same wages and apparently were going to be subject to slave codes modified only in name. They had been freed practically with no land nor money, and, save in exceptional circumstances, without legal status, and without protection.[3]

A white Tennessean put it bluntly: "Nigger life's cheap now. When a white man feels aggrieved at anything a nigger's done, he just shoots him and puts an end to it." In the face of such conditions, Republicans were divided over what should be done. Radicals called for federal intervention. "The same national authority that destroyed slavery must see that this other pretension is not permitted to survive," said the Radicals' leader in the Senate, the long-time abolitionist Charles Sumner of Massachusetts.[4] Moderates were inclined to give Johnson more time. They were also wary of the political costs of a too-ardent support for black rights. Even so, they agreed to establish a Joint Committee on Reconstruction that would report on conditions in the South and make policy recommendations to the full Congress.

Senator Charles Sumner of Massachusetts (1811–1874). (Library of Congress)

Testimony before the Joint Committee in early 1866 convinced many moderates that the Johnson policy had failed. Witness after witness provided evidence of the systematic abuse of former slaves. (Only eight blacks were called as witnesses. Several former Confederates testified, among them ex-vice president Stephens, who spoke in favor of slavery.) Against this backdrop, moderates joined with Radicals in February 1866 to pass a bill to extend the life of the

Freedmen's Bureau and, for the first time, provide direct funding for bureau operations. A few weeks later, the Republican majority, as a counter to the Black Codes, approved a civil rights bill assuring "full and equal benefit of the laws" without regard to race. During the war, Charles Sumner had fought for equal pay for black soldiers. He had campaigned successfully to end discrimination on District of Columbia streetcars, and unsuccessfully for the right of District blacks to vote. He was an eloquent champion of equality before the law. "This is the Great Guarantee," Sumner said, "without which all other guarantees will fail."[5] Still, the civil rights measure had not mentioned black suffrage, an essential component of emancipation so far as Radicals were concerned. Nor did Congress, in early 1866, take up the issue of economic independence for the freed people.

Sumner's Radical ally in the House, Thaddeus Stevens, lobbied hard for the vote and for land reform as primary elements of a sweeping reorganization of the Southern system. The planter class, Stevens believed, had to be destroyed: "How can republican institutions, free schools, free churches, free social intercourse, exist in a mingled community of nabobs and serfs?"[6] He proposed a massive program of land confiscation that would break up the great estates and enable the government to grant a homestead to every freed family.

In some ways, Stevens was more a visionary than a practical politician. ("No man was oftener outvoted," a journalist once said of him.) Stevens himself acknowledged the revolutionary nature of his views, but made no apology for them. His response to those who could not or would not keep pace with him could be withering. Of his call for a social revolution in the South, Stevens said:

This may startle feeble minds and shake weak nerves. So do all great improvements in the political and moral world. It requires a heavy impetus to drive forward a sluggish people. When it was first proposed to free the slaves, and arm the blacks, did not half the nation tremble? The prim conservatives, the snobs, and the male waiting maids in Congress were in hysterics.[7]

Initially, the full Congress disappointed Sumner and Stevens on the suffrage question. In tabling the issue, the moderates hoped to avoid a complete break with the president, who had revealed himself to be an implacable enemy of full citizenship for former slaves. But that was before Johnson, in the first months of 1866, vetoed both the Freedmen's Bureau and the civil rights bills. The vetoes drove congressional moderates and Radicals into alliance, isolated the president, and doomed his reconstruction program. The Republicans mustered the two-thirds majority necessary to override the civil rights veto and eventually approved, over yet another Johnson veto, a second measure extending the bureau's life.

Then, in early April, congressional Republicans drafted a constitutional amendment that was intended to guarantee equal protection under the law. The Fourteenth Amendment also mandated a reduction in congressional representation in proportion to the number of male citizens denied the vote. And it disenfranchised certain classes of high Confederate officials for several years, giving the new democratic order time to establish itself.

Senator Henry Wilson, Sumner's Massachusetts colleague, offered this rationale for the congressional actions of the winter and spring of 1866:

We must see to it that the man made free by the Constitution is a freeman indeed; that he can go where he pleases, work when and for whom he pleases; that he can sue or be sued; that he can lease and buy and sell and own property, real and personal; that he can go into the schools and educate himself and his children; that the rights and guarantees of the common law are his, and that he walks the earth proud and erect in the conscious dignity of a free man.[8]

The Fourteenth Amendment's provisions seemed modest enough in the circumstances; some Radicals, in fact, were disappointed in its failure to explicitly guarantee black suffrage. Said Frederick Douglass: "To tell me that I am an equal American citizen, and, in the same breath, tell me that my right to vote may be constitutionally taken from me by some other equal citizen or citizens, is to tell me that my citizenship is an empty name."[9] Most Radicals, though, believed that they had little choice but to support the measure, and it passed in June 1866.

President Johnson chose to campaign against ratification. There was, the president insisted, no need for such an amendment. Wrote DuBois: "He declared in the face of an astounding array of testimony to the contrary that the South was peaceful and loyal, and the slaves really free."[10] Johnson viewed the measure, accurately, as a threat to white supremacy. Southerners needed little encouragement to follow his lead. With the exception of Tennessee, every state of the old Confederacy rejected the amendment.

If Northerners required additional evidence of the need for federal guarantees, events in the South soon supplied it. In Memphis, Tennessee, in early May, white policemen joined white mobs in a rampage through black neighborhoods. At least 46 blacks were killed and hundreds of black homes, churches, and schools were damaged or destroyed. "Thank heaven the white race are once more rulers of Memphis," a local newspaper editor wrote in the wake of the riot.[11] In late July in New Orleans, white police opened fire on a political meeting of blacks and their white Republican allies, killing 37 people (34 of them black) and wounding more than a hundred.

Northern newspapers gave the riots extensive coverage, and the reports caused widespread revulsion. "The hands of rebels are again red with loyal blood," the *New York Tribune* charged.[12] In off-year balloting in the autumn of 1866, Northern voters remembered the mob outrages, and in what was in effect a referendum on the Johnson reconstruction program, they gave congressional Republicans an overwhelming victory. With majorities greater than two thirds in both Houses, the Republicans would be virtually veto-proof in 1867.

The 1866 vote set the stage for the Radical phase of Reconstruction. Congress moved rapidly to take control of the government's policies. By the end of 1866 most moderates had come around in support of black suffrage, though it had been a close call and the often-exasperated Radicals had sometimes fallen back on humor laced with sarcasm to make their points. Radical representative George Julian of Indiana took the floor to oppose a move to impose educational tests on voting-age blacks:

> Reading and writing are mechanical processes, and a man may be able to perform them without any worthiness of life or character. If penmanship must be made the avenue to the ballot, I fear several honorable gentlemen on this floor will be disenfranchised.[13]

In part, the moderates responded to a powerful political argument that only African-American votes would ensure continued Republican dominance. The destruction of slavery meant the end of the "three-fifths" rule, that odd, illogical compromise established in the Constitution by which only 60 percent of the slave population had been counted in figuring the South's congressional representation. Henceforth, all freedmen would be counted whether they voted or not, giving the South greater power in Congress and in the Electoral College than it had exercised before the war. Apart from its effects on the freed people, a white Democratic South would imperil the Republican economic program of high tariffs to protect Northern industry, low interest rates, aid to railroads, and a generous homestead lands policy in the West.

"If [black] suffrage is excluded in the rebel states then every one of them is sure to send a solid rebel representative delegation to Congress," Stevens warned.[14]

So the prospect of an alliance of a solid South with northern Democrats lent urgency to the Republican program. On March 2, 1867, the first Reconstruction Act reached the president's desk. It divided 10 Southern states (Tennessee had approved the Fourteenth Amendment and was exempt) into five military districts. The act and its supplements enfranchised the freedmen and required the states to adopt constitutions guaranteeing universal male suffrage. (Women would continue to be denied the vote until 1920.) To qualify for readmission, the states also would have to ratify the Fourteenth Amendment.

Johnson vetoed the Reconstruction Act. Congress overrode him and the bill became law. With final enactment, a milestone in the nation's history had been reached. Weary and relieved, congressional Republicans hoped for the best. "The legislation of the last two years will mark a great page of history for good or evil—I hope the former," said Senator Waitman T. Willey of West Virginia.[15]

The turn of events energized Southern black Republican leaders. "We are determined to secure our rights," Francis Cardozo told an assembly in Charleston, South Carolina in late March. "The noble men of [the Republican Party] have battled for your rights, and have been triumphant over foes and pretended friends." Cardozo finished up with a plea for support of the party of the freed people: "Do you not owe them a debt of gratitude?"[16]

Senator Willey issued a warning: "The crisis is not yet past."[17] That would prove all too true; though for the moment the legislation gave rise to new hope that the postwar system of slavery by another name might finally be overthrown. In several Southern ports, poorly paid black dockworkers tested the new conditions by going on strike. In Richmond, Charleston, and New Orleans, blacks protested discrimination on streetcar lines. In South Carolina, several hundred blacks refused to pay taxes to the soon-to-be-dismantled Johnson state government.

Throughout the South, African-American communities hummed with political activity. Schools, churches, and other organizations became politicized. "Politics got in our midst and our revival or religious work for a while began to wane," one black parson recalled.[18] In Washington, the Republican Congressional Committee funded tours by some 80 "colored itinerant lecturers," who helped kindle political passions in town after Southern town.

New or revived chapters of the Union League and other patriotic societies served as the freedmen's political forum. "We just went there," a North Carolina Union Leaguer recalled, "and we talked a little; made speeches on one question or another."[19] The chapters also supported black schools and churches and raised money to aid the sick and indigent. Some Texas Union Leaguers campaigned for back pay for people held in slavery after the Emancipation Proclamation.

League activists formed part of the expanding black leadership. Georgia Union League organizer Thomas Allen, a Baptist preacher and shoemaker, commanded wide influence in his county. Allen's power grew out of his ability to read. "The colored people came to me for instruction, and I gave them the best instructions I could," he recalled. "I took the *New York Tribune* and other papers, and in that way I found out a great deal, and I told them whatever I thought was right."[20] Working with Northern volunteers, soldiers, and Freedmen's Bureau agents, Allen and other Union Leaguers registered thousands of voters during the summer of 1867.

"We are not prepared for this suffrage," conceded South Carolinian Beverly C. Nash, a former slave. "But we can learn. Give a man tools and let him commence to use them, and in time he will learn a trade. So it is with voting."[21]

Altogether, nearly 1.4 million Southerners were registered to vote in the former Confederate states—735,000 blacks and 635,000 whites. Blacks outnumbered whites in South Carolina, Florida, Alabama, Mississippi, and Louisiana. Past service to the Confederacy barred an estimated 150,000 whites from registering.

Most whites reacted predictably. But even in their outrage, some white Southerners realized they had only themselves to blame for the reimposition of military rule and for renewed federal guarantees of black civil rights. Northern traveler John Trowbridge asked a white Mississippian whether he thought his state's Johnson legislature had miscalculated in adopting the restrictive Black Codes. "Yes," he replied. "It was unwise *at this time. We showed our hand too soon.*"[22]

Whites experienced fear as well as anger. The merest rumor of weapons in black hands set off alarms of race war. Yet throughout the postwar period the freed people committed remarkably little violence against whites. Far more often, there were pleas for racial peace. In a petition to Governor Humphries, Mississippi freedmen sought relief from the Black Codes, not revenge.

> We do not want our rights by murdering. We owe too much to many of our white friends that has shown us mercy in bygone days to harm them. Some of us wish Mr. Jeff Davis to be set at liberty for we know worse masters than he was. Altho he tried hard to keep us in slavery we forgive him.[23]

Increasingly, though, black leaders let it be known that their patience had limits. In a petition for redress to the Georgia legislature, Augusta blacks reminded whites of the forbearance they had shown during the war, when most of the young white men were away and slaves had the power to "fire your houses, burn your homes and railroads and discommode you in a thousand ways."[24] The petition went on to assert that the freed people would not quietly acquiesce in continued abridgements of their newfound freedom. In each state the old Confederacy, voters elected multiracial conventions whose delegates met to draw up new constitutions affirming black suffrage and equality before the law. Blacks formed a majority in two conventions, those of Louisiana and South Carolina. Convention delegates were a mix of carpetbaggers (Northerners drawn south by climate, opportunity, or conscience), scalawags (Southern white Republicans), former slaves, and freeborn blacks. Out of a total of 1,000 delegates to the several state conventions, 265 were black. So far as is known, 107 had been born into slavery. Fewer than 30 were Northerners. Some 40 were Union army veterans. Clergymen were much in evidence—17 of Georgia's 22 black delegates were churchmen.

Carpetbaggers generally ran the conventions. Together, newly enfranchised blacks and their allies produced constitutions that, on paper anyway, were models of fairness. They established the South's first state-funded school systems. Some made provisions for social services, including relief for the poor. Within a year or so, eight states had organized governments under the new constitutions, submitted the constitutions for voter approval, ratified the Fourteenth Amendment, and elected local and state officials.

Still, as Senator Willey had suggested, the issue was far from being decided. "These constitutions and these governments will last just as long as the bayonets which ushered them into being shall keep them in existence," a Democratic newspaper asserted.[25] In Washington, the battle between the president and Congress continued to escalate. Johnson used his authority as commander in chief of the army to blunt the impact of Reconstruction. In August 1867 he dismissed War Secretary Edwin M. Stanton—the sole surviving Radical in the cabinet. Johnson also

Andrew Johnson (1808–1875), 17th president of the United States. (Library of Congress)

replaced several senior army commanders sympathetic to congressional Reconstruction, including Philip Sheridan, Daniel Sickles, John Pope, and Edward O. C. Ord. Sheridan in particular ran afoul of the president for breaking up gangs

Freedom's Champion

By 1865, Frederick Douglass had emerged as the unchallenged national spokesman for African Americans. Born enslaved in Maryland, he had bolted for freedom and risen to become one of the most influential leaders of the abolition movement. With the coming of emancipation, Douglass campaigned tirelessly for the extension of black civil and political rights.

Proud, remote, somewhat touchy, Douglass put his faith in equality before the law rather than Northern good will as the chief guarantor of black advancement. His views of the Northern charitable organizations—many leaders of which were longtime abolition allies—were ambivalent, to put it mildly.

"The Negro needs justice more than pity, liberty more than old clothes," he wrote J. Miller McKim, the head of one of the most important of the charity agencies, the American Freedmen's Aid Society.[29]

Douglass reserved his most intensive efforts for black suffrage. "Without the elective franchise, the Negro will still practically be a slave," he

of the "white banditti" who had renewed the terror campaign against blacks in Louisiana.

Election results across the nation in the autumn of 1867 encouraged Johnson and his conservative allies. Republicans ran well in the South, where black turnout ranged as high as 90 percent. "The negroes voted their entire walking strength—no one staying at home that was able to come to the polls," remarked a white Alabama Republican. But in the North, the Democrats shamelessly played the race card. Noted the visiting French journalist (and future premier) Georges Clemenceau: "Any Democrat who did not manage to hint in his speech that the Negro is a degenerate gorilla would be considered lacking in enthusiasm."[26] Democrats found the tactic effective. They recorded substantial gains in argued. "Individual ownership has been abolished, but if we restore the Southern states without this measure, we shall establish an ownership of the blacks by the community among whom they live."[30] In the long term, the ballot, not federal garrisons, would assure protection and progress for the freed people.

At a White House meeting in February 1866, Douglass found President Johnson so hostile to the idea of black suffrage that the matter could scarcely be discussed. Whites and blacks voting together, the president predicted, would touch off a race war. Douglass, however, could count on powerful allies among the Radical Republicans in Congress. Senator Charles Sumner, Representative Thaddeus Stevens and others responded instinctively to one of Douglass's most telling arguments. In a monarchy, Douglass said, the few ruled the many and nearly all were excluded. Not so in the United States:

> Where universal suffrage is the fundamental idea of the government, to rule us out is to make us an exception, to brand us with the stigma of inferiority.[31] ◆

several Northern states. White voters in Ohio, Minnesota, and Kansas emphatically rejected black suffrage.

Thus emboldened, Johnson risked a final confrontation with Congress. The Senate reinstated Stanton, citing the Radical-inspired Tenure of Office Act, which barred the president from removing officials whose politics displeased him. Johnson tempted fate by dismissing the war secretary a second time. In retaliation, the House passed a resolution of impeachment on February 24, 1868, instructing the Senate to try Johnson for violating the tenure law and for bringing "the high office of the President of the United States into contempt, ridicule and disgrace."

After an eight-week trial, Johnson narrowly avoided a conviction. With moderate Republicans wavering, the Senate on May 26, 1868 fell a single vote short of the two-thirds majority necessary to remove him from office. The decisions of a handful of moderates enabled the accidental president to finish out his term, which ended on March 4, 1869.

In November 1868, black votes helped to elect Republican Ulysses S. Grant to the presidency. The implications could not have been clearer to the freed people. "The blacks know that many conservatives hope to reduce them again to some form of peonage," a Tennessee carpetbagger explained. "Under the impulse of this fear they will roll up their whole strength and will go entirely for the Republican candidate, whoever he may be."[27] As they had in 1867, African Americans turned out in massive numbers.

It was an ugly, violent campaign. Republicans continually reminded the voters who had brought on the Civil War. "Scratch a Democrat and you find a rebel under the skin," Republican candidates claimed. In the South, the secret organizations—Sheridan's "banditti"—conducted a campaign of murder and arson. The Ku Klux Klan, a secret society of white supremacist former Confederate soldiers, carried out guerrilla warfare in nearly every Southern state. "Beware," ran one of the Klan's weird threats, "thy end is nigh. Dead, dead under the roses."[28] There were hundreds of political murders. An Arkansas congressman and three South Carolina legislators were assassinated. White mobs broke up Republican meetings. In many locales, armed groups of whites turned blacks away from the polls.

The new Republican state governments were still too weak to stop the violence. The army garrisons too were ineffective. Only 20,000 U.S. troops were available to police the entire South, and in any case many of Johnson's military appointees shared his views on black rights. Sheridan's successor in Louisiana went so far as to urge blacks to stay home on election day as a matter of self-preservation.

Even though Grant won a substantial Electoral College victory, he outpolled his Democratic opponent by only 300,000 votes out of 5.7 million cast. Nationwide, the

Democratic candidate probably took a majority of the white vote. Newly enfranchised Southern blacks thus provided President Grant's winning margin.

NOTES

1. Eric Foner, *Reconstruction: America's Unfinished Revolution, 1863–1877* (New York: Harper & Row, 1988), 240.

2. Kenneth M. Stampp, *The Era of Reconstruction, 1865–1877* (New York: Alfred A. Knopf, 1965), 51.

3. W. E. B. DuBois, *Black Reconstruction in America* (New York: Russell & Russell, 1962), 188.

4. First quote, Leon F. Litwack, *Been in the Storm So Long: The Aftermath of Slavery* (New York: Alfred A. Knopf, 1979), 275; second quote, Foner, *Reconstruction*, 232.

5. DuBois, *Black Reconstruction*, 193.

6. DuBois, *Black Reconstruction*, 197.

7. Stampp, *The Era of Reconstruction*, 104.

8. Stampp, *The Era of Reconstruction*, 88.

9. James M. McPherson, *The Struggle for Equality: Abolitionists and the Negro in the Civil War and Reconstruction* (Princeton, N.J.: Princeton University Press, 1965), 355.

10. DuBois, *Black Reconstruction*, 277.

11. Rembert W. Patrick, *Reconstruction of the Nation*, (New York: Oxford University Press, 1967), 83.

12. Patrick, *Reconstruction of the Nation*, 85.

13. Stampp, *The Era of Reconstruction*, 143.

14. Stampp, *The Era of Reconstruction*, 93.

15. Foner, *Reconstruction*, 280.

16. Herbert Aptheker, ed., *A Documentary History of the Negro in the United States*, Volume 1, 56.

17. Foner, *Reconstruction*, 280.

18. Foner, *Reconstruction*, 282.

19. Foner, *Reconstruction*, 284.

20. Foner, *Reconstruction*, 287.

21. Patrick, *Reconstruction of the Nation*, 115.

22. John T. Trowbridge, *The South: A Tour of Its Battlefields and Ruined Cities* (New York: Arno Press, 1969 reprint), 373.

23. Litwack, *Been in the Storm*, 201.

24. DuBois, *Black Reconstruction*, 232.

25. Foner, *Reconstruction*, 333.

26. First quote, Foner, *Reconstruction*; second quote, Georges Clemenceau, *American Reconstruction*, Fernand Baldensperger, ed.; Margaret MacVeagh, trans. (New York: Da Capo Press, 1969), 131.

27. Stampp, *The Era of Reconstruction*, 166.

28. Richard W. Murphy, *The Nation Reunited: War's Aftermath* (Alexandria, Va.: Time-Life Books, 1987), 76, 97.

29. William S. McFeely, *Frederick Douglass* (New York: W. W. Norton, 1991), 241.

30. McFeely, *Frederick Douglass*, 246.

31. Foner, *Reconstruction*, 75.

6

Radical Rule: 1868–1874

The South's Reconstruction governments faced formidable challenges in 1868. Most state economies were in disarray, depressed by the aftershocks of war, the uncertainties of emancipation, and poor cotton harvests in 1866 and 1867. State treasuries were empty. The ruling Republicans struggled to establish the authority of the new governments and to accelerate the process of social and economic reconstruction. Conservative Southern whites remained unalterably hostile to the rise of the freed people and to their carpetbagger and scalawag allies.

In two states of the old Confederacy, Radical Reconstruction never got off the ground. The collapse came early in

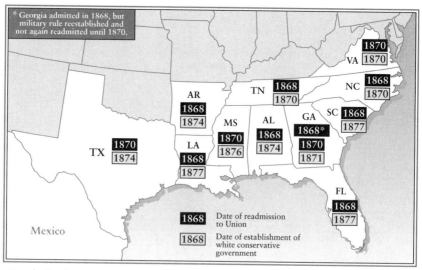

VA 1870 / 1870

TN 1868 / 1870

NC 1868 / 1870

AR 1868 / 1874

MS 1870 / 1876

AL 1868 / 1874

GA 1868* / 1870 / 1871

SC 1868 / 1877

TX 1870 / 1874

LA 1868 / 1877

FL 1868 / 1877

Mexico

1868 Date of readmission to Union

1868 Date of establishment of white conservative government

Readmitted states.

Georgia, where in September 1868, with the assistance of some white Republicans, Democrats expelled black members of the state legislature. Virginians were more subtle. A coalition of Democrats and conservative Republicans acknowledged black suffrage, renounced organized efforts to keep blacks from the polls, and won the governorship in 1869. In that election African Americans cast 100,000 of the 225,000 ballots, the largest turnout in Virginia history up to then; 27 blacks won election to the state legislature. By contrast, conservative Republicans in alliance with Democrats gained power in Tennessee in 1869 by ignoring the suffrage law and enrolling disenfranchised Confederates.

The Radical-inspired Fifteenth Amendment, ratified early in 1870, prohibited state governments from denying or abridging voting rights "on account of race, color or previous condition of servitude." From the first, though, some Southern state legislatures schemed to subvert the amendment. Tennessee introduced a poll tax (a tax on voters) that effectively barred African Americans from voting. Maryland, a former slave state that had remained loyal during the Civil

War, adopted a property qualification that kept many blacks from the polls.

Even in states where the Radicals were ascendant, there were signs of discord. Historian Eric Foner summarized the divisions among Southern Republicans, Radical and moderate, Northern and native-born, black and white:

> Republicans achieved far greater agreement on general principles than their actual implementation: on public education but not whether schools should be racially integrated; civil and political rights for blacks but not 'social equality'; the expansion of democracy but not the disenfranchisement of rebels; economic modernization, but not how to balance the need for outside capital with white farmers' demands for debtor relief and blacks' for land.[1]

The whites who controlled Republican Party organizations in all the states in the first years of Radical Reconstruction worked hard to court native white voters, often using patronage as an enticement. Blacks expecting a fair proportion of offices and political plums resented this. Intraparty squabbling, often over the spoils of office, created political opportunities for opposition Democrats. "We must keep together, scalawags, carpetbaggers and niggers," a North Carolina Republican pleaded.[2] Still, the new party organizations too often lacked the discipline to hold ranks against the common foe.

Some black leaders went along at first with Republican attempts to build a voter base among native whites—efforts that usually involved reserving the most powerful offices for whites. Martin Delany, the Freedman's Bureau agent, declined to run for a South Carolina congressional seat in 1868 to avoid antagonizing whites. For the same reason, the state's black-majority legislature chose a white Speaker of the House. More than half the citizens of Natchez, Mississippi were black, but African Americans at no time held more than three of the seven seats on the city council. The big federal and state patronage offices generally went to whites, too, with small-town postmasterships and other less lucrative offices distributed to blacks.

In the main, then, whites ruled, confirmed in power by black votes. In some states, most notably Mississippi and South Carolina, black and white Republicans generally worked together in harmony. In June 1870, Mississippi's Reconstruction legislature, which included 40 black senators and representatives (out of a total of around 140 members), repealed the repressive Slave Code of 1857 and nearly all of the Black Code of 1865. Mississippi legislators aimed at the eventual elimination of all state laws that discriminated on the basis of race.

Black political leadership continued to develop, and in some states blacks wielded real power. In Mississippi, where 30 of the 72 counties had African-American majorities, Union (or Loyal) Leaguers, closely allied with the Republican Party, provided a core leadership—often, especially in the early days, dominated by preachers, lawyers, and teachers from the free states or Canada. Of the native-born leaders, the majority had been urban slaves with artisan skills—blacksmiths, carpenters, clerks, and the like.

In Florida, a carpetbagger noted in 1868, black clergymen strongly influenced the political behavior of the freed people. "The colored preachers are *the great power* in controlling and uniting the colored vote, and they are looked to, as political leaders, with more confidence than to any other source of instruction and control," he wrote. In South Carolina, the Civil War celebrity Robert Smalls ruled over political life in the Port Royal region, where after a brief struggle former slaves had taken control of the local Republican organization from white Northern missionaries and cotton superintendents. "There has been an effort to form a Republican party, but it has not succeeded very well yet," the

A group of freedmen listen to a campaign speech in this wood engraving from Harper's Weekly *of July 25, 1868. Blacks turned out heavily for Reconstruction-era elections and voted overwhelmingly Republican.* (Library of Congress)

Gideonite T. Edwin Ruggles had written in 1867. "They [the freedmen] are too suspicious to be led by whites."[3] Once the whites gave way, the party flourished. By 1873, the mayor, the police force, and all the magistrates of Beaufort, Smalls's overwhelmingly Republican hometown, were black.

Elsewhere, the Republicans' hold on power could be precarious, their security uncertain. Conservative whites boycotted Republican merchants, lawyers, and planters. This led to the establishment of a class of public officials completely dependent on reelection or party patronage for a livelihood. "I do not know what I shall do," wrote a New Orleans scalawag who had lost his political job as a weights and measures inspector. "My own relatives have turned their backs and it will be impossible for me to get any employment."[4]

In some places, whites used their economic power to try to drive blacks out of public life. "I always had plenty of work before I went into politics," remarked bricklayer Henry Johnson, an upcountry South Carolina legislator, "but I have never got a job since. I suppose they do it merely because they think they will break me down and keep me from interfering with politics." Blacks might be dismissed from work merely for voting Republican. "We are gratified to learn that one hundred and fifty negroes employed at the Wythe Iron Mines, all of whom voted the straight radical ticket, were discharged on Tuesday by the owner of the mine," the *Lynchburg* (Virginia) *News* reported in 1869.[5] Most states experienced a high turnover of black officeholders from election to election, most likely because of the economic hardships that increasingly became associated with Republican public service.

Despite the difficulties, the new Republican governments could claim substantive achievements. Prewar Southern state governments had provided the barest minimum of services. "It is said that the antebellum state was ruled by 180 great landlords," W. E. B. DuBois wrote of South Carolina. "They made the functions of the state just as few as possible, and did by private law on private plantations most of the things which in other states were carried on by the local and state governments."[6] Reconstruction regimes funded public school systems, built asylums, orphanages and prisons, paved roads, provided relief for the poor, and promoted railroad development and other internal improvements. Spending and taxes rose sharply—South Carolina's state budget doubled between 1860 and 1873—but many Southerners, especially African Americans, could count real benefits from government's activist role.

Few of the new school systems that emerged after the Civil War were integrated, though, except in New Orleans, where for several years in the 1870s black and white children attended school together. Finances were a problem, too.

After 1868, Northern charitable societies began to curtail their involvement. Before it went out of existence in 1872, the Freedmen's Bureau spent some $16 million on the education of former slaves. When the federal government passed on this burden to the states and localities, results were decidedly mixed. In Savannah, Georgia, for instance, the school board in 1873 spent $64,000 on white schools, $3,000 on black schools.

Nevertheless, most African Americans felt that separate schools were better than no schools at all. By the early 1870s, newly established black colleges—Fisk in Tennessee, Alcorn in Mississippi, Howard in Washington, among others—were turning out hundreds of black teachers (and other professionals) every year. In South Carolina, the number of black teachers, many of them graduates of the new black colleges, rose from 50 in 1869 to 1,000 in 1875.

One by one, the Republican legislatures struck the last remnants of the Black Codes from the books. In some states, officials made good-faith efforts to end segregation in public places and in restaurants, hotels, streetcars, and steamboats. Unfortunately, such initiatives only served to deepen the divisions in the Republican Party. "I am willing to give the Negro political and civil rights, but social equality, never," declared a South Carolina scalawag legislator. After one such declaration, a black South Carolinian replied coolly: "I for one do not ask to be introduced into your family circle if you are not disposed to receive me there." In Mississippi, Reconstruction governor James L. Alcorn intended, according to one observer, to "harness" the black revolution, his purpose to see "the old civilization of the South *modernized*."[7] Alcorn supported suffrage for blacks, but adamantly opposed legislative efforts to promote social equality.

Nor were the Radical state regimes any more effective than the federal government had been in advancing blacks' economic prospects. In 1867, the Radical representative Thaddeus Stevens had failed to gain support in Congress for his proposal to grant a 40-acre homestead and $50 in cash to every freedman head of a family. This practically ended Congress's involvement in the matter. No state launched a comprehensive land reform program; there were no confiscations of white estates to aid landless blacks, no homestead measures tailored to black settlers.

True, the Homestead Act of 1866 had opened 46 million acres of public lands in Florida, Alabama, Mississippi, and Arkansas. The intent was to make cheap land available to freed people—but the effect was negligible. Typically, the offerings were poor—swamplands or bleak rocky uplands bypassed by earlier white settlers. In any case, few blacks had the capital—mules, implements, seed—to make an independent start. In a decade, only about 2,000 black families were settled on homestead lands in the Southern states.

In a partial exception to the rule, South Carolina pursued a modest program of land distribution during the first half of the 1870s. The state legislature established a commission to acquire farmland and sell it to freed people on easy credit terms. By 1876, some 14,000 black families—or about one family in every seven—had obtained homesteads of 25 to 100 acres through the South Carolina land agency.

In other states, Republican leaders evidently hoped that rising taxes on land would encourage planters to put surplus or uncultivated holdings on the market. Some called for taxing very large landowners at the steep rate of $1 per acre. Tax defaulters would see their property sold to the highest bidder, one possible means of promoting black landownership. Taxes were raised in many places, but it rarely worked out as planned. In Mississippi, in fact, the original owners eventually regained 95 percent of the land forfeited for nonpayment of taxes.

Reconstruction legislators did, however, enact laws that granted some protection to laboring people, especially farm workers. Most states rebuffed planters' demands to retain aspects of the old system of labor control. In Southern courtooms, black magistrates and black juries refused to automatically accept planters' interpretations of labor contracts. "Justice," one planter complained, "is generally administered solely in the interest of the laborer."[8] In South Carolina, workers' wages could not be seized for debt, nor could a planter remove his crop before the field hands had been fully paid off.

With the failure of land reform, the system known as sharecropping gradually took hold in the South. Under this system, the landowner provided acreage, a dwelling, a team, tools, and seed, while the cropper supplied the labor. At harvest time, owner and laborer divided the crop, usually in half. The freed people endorsed sharecropping as a form of economic autonomy—they were not working for wages, and they were masters of their own time. There was another benefit, one that many blacks valued beyond price. Sharecropping led to the breakup of the old slave quarters. Laboring families most often lived away by themselves in scattered cabins, usually close to the plots of land they worked.

Many whites resisted the new arrangement. "Wages are the only successful system of controlling hands," one planter wrote. Nevertheless, by the early 1870s sharecropping had become the chief form of black labor. In time, this meant trouble for all concerned. Small merchants set up shop at every dusty crossroads of the rural South, eager to sell to this new class of semi-independent farmers. The new consumers required credit, however. A sharecropper needed to borrow for food and other necessities to see him through the long growing season. Interest rates were high and cheating was common. "A man that didn't know how to count would always lose," an Arkansas freedman remarked.[9] After tapping his share to pay off his debts, a cropper usually had little left, even in bumper years.

In bad crop years, merchants had little choice but to carry over debts from one autumn to the next. "The credit system has been pushed to such an extent that crops have been mortgaged for supplies before they have been planted," a white Mississippi planter observed. Perceptive black farmers recognized the dangers of the system. "No man can work another man's land and make any money," said one. "The freedmen will become poorer and poorer every year."[10] And so it turned out. Most sharecroppers found themselves caught in a recurring cycle of debt.

The landlord/merchant class knew hard times too. Sharecropping led to a destructive overproduction of the cash crop. When that happened, soils were exhausted, cotton markets were glutted, prices were depressed. In poor harvest years, or when cotton prices were low, misery knew no class or racial boundaries. But even during the palmiest days of Radical Reconstruction, sharecroppers generally found that commercial law and custom operated against them. In many states, crop lien laws guaranteed that the proceeds of the harvest would go first to lenders of credit or supplies. So when a landowner failed to pay *his* debts, his tenants got no share of the crop.

Radical government survived longest in the two states with the largest black populations, South Carolina and Mississippi. South Carolina, in fact, became the only state in which African Americans, who made up more than half the state's population, attained a majority in the legislature. There, as noted, Republican governments built a system of public education from the ground up—South Carolina's school population quadrupled, from 30,000 students in 1868 to 123,000 in 1876. They saw to improvements in a broad range of state services. They reformed the judicial system from top to bottom, and opened all judicial offices to blacks.

Long after the end of Radical Reconstruction, in a powerful speech before South Carolina's white supremacist legislature, black legislator Thomas Miller assessed the state's brief era of interracial rule:

We were eight years in power. We had built school-houses, established charitable institutions, built and maintained the penitentiary system, provided for the education of the deaf and dumb, rebuilt the jails and courthouses, rebuilt the bridges and reestablished the ferries. In short, we had reconstructed the state and placed it on the road to prosperity.[11]

The gains came, however, at the price of heavy taxation and widespread corruption. "I hoped to make money—dreamed of thousands," South Carolina's carpet-bagger governor Daniel Chamberlain confessed to a friend.[12] Senior Republican leaders floated fraudulent bonds, raked off thousands from dubious state loans to railroads and sales of state-owned railroad stock, and solic-ited bribes from railroad speculators and other promoters. Officials demanded and received large payoffs for granting business charters and franchises.

As most modern historians have emphasized, thieves, buc-caneers, and spoilsmen operated at all levels of government, in the North as well as in the South. Though President Grant seems to have been personally honest, his administration has gone down as one of the most corrupt in American history. "Grantism" became a byword for graft. "Thirteen relations of the President are billeted on the country," Senator Charles Sumner remarked acidly, in reference to Grant kinsmen who had been eased into high-paying public jobs. "There is hardly a legislature in the country which is not suspected of corrup-tion," *The Nation* lamented.[13] In New York City, the noto-rious Tweed Ring stole more than all the Radical Republican governments combined.

In the South as elsewhere, corruption was bipartisan. "You are mistaken if you suppose that all the evils result from the carpetbaggers and negroes—the Democrats are leagued with them when anything is proposed which promises to pay," a Louisiana conservative said. As a

John Roy Lynch, a Louisana-born former slave, represented Mississippi in the U.S. Congress into the 1880s. (New York Public Library)

matter of common practice, Northern carpetbaggers and native scalawags were the bolder and more ambitious thieves. Scalawag Franklin K. Moses, a member of the old South Carolina planter class turned Republican, plundered without restraint after he became governor in 1872. Massachusetts-born carpetbagger Daniel Chamberlain, Moses's successor, stole more discreetly—a "shrewd and able" politician, DuBois judged him, "but not overly scrupulous." Dishonest freedmen ordinarily contented themselves with modest gains. "I was pretty hard up, and I did not care who the candidate was if I got two hundred dollars," one black South Carolina legislator said, explaining the sale of his vote for a U.S. Senate seat.[14] By contrast, the Democratic treasurer of Mississippi's first post-Radical white supremacist government made off with $315,000—more than the total of all the thieving during six years of Republican rule.

Historians agree that Radical Republicans provided Mississippi with the most efficient and honest government of the Reconstruction era. Black voters commanded substantial influence there. The election of 1871 returned 66 Republicans to the lower house of the legislature, a comfortable majority. The party's 38-member African-American contingent overrode white opposition to choose John Lynch as Speaker.

Two years later, the Republicans reached the zenith of their power in Mississippi. This came, ironically, at a time when black demands for a larger share of political offices had split the party in two. James Alcorn, the scalawag planter and first Republican governor, had served briefly in the U.S. Senate, then returned to Mississippi to try to reclaim the governorship at the head of a conservative white faction. Most native white Republicans supported Alcorn, who also picked up Democratic backing. Blacks rallied behind carpetbagger Adelbert Ames, a former Union general from Maine.

Ames had convinced himself, he wrote long afterward, that he "had a Mission with a large M" to help former slaves attain full citizenship.[15] With the help of a heavy black turnout, Ames handily defeated Alcorn, whose plantation hands were even said to have voted against him. African Americans captured 55 of the 115 seats in the lower House, nine of 37 Senate seats, and three of the top seven statewide offices, including the lieutenant governorship and the superintendency of education.

Higher Learning for the Emancipated Generation_____

Benjamin Holmes enrolled at the Fisk Free School in Nashville, Tennessee in 1868 to prepare himself to teach. Born enslaved in South Carolina, sold early in 1863, and sent to Chattanooga, Tennessee, he became free with the arrival of federal forces later in the year. A tailor by trade, Holmes had been a servant to a Yankee general and a barber's clerk before entering Fisk.

Two American Missionary Society officials and a Freedmen's Bureau agent established Fisk in 1866 to be a primary school, a training ground for black teachers and, ultimately, a top-rank liberal arts college. Fisk built upon what its founders termed a broad Christian foundation. In many ways, Benjamin Holmes seemed a typical Fisk student. He studied "history, Latin, practice of teaching and analysis" and served as a deacon of the Fisk church.[17]

Holmes found a teaching job in a freedmen's school eight miles outside Nashville. He returned to the Fisk campus on Friday nights for meetings of the literary society, and on Saturdays he plied his tailor's trade to supplement his $30 a month salary. Every Sabbath, he taught a Sunday-school class. "I lacked neither work nor exercise," Holmes told an interviewer in 1872.[18]

Fisk accepted the first students in its new college department in 1871. But like most Reconstruction-era black institutions, the university nearly

Ames took office, however, at an inauspicious time. In September 1873, the failure of the banking firm of Jay Gould and Company touched off a financial crisis that plunged the country into a severe depression. The Panic of 1873 threw nearly a million people out of work. Thousands of businesses failed. One railroad in every four went bankrupt.

In larger terms, the depression turned the nation's attention away from the problems of Reconstruction. It also lent more urgency to conservatives' attacks on corruption in foundered for lack of books, equipment, and money. In late 1871, the school's treasurer, desperate for a moneymaking scheme, organized a group of student singers and set out on a fund-raising tour of the Midwest.

The Fisk Jubilee Singers became an instant hit. Their repertoire of spirituals and other songs they had learned as slaves drew enthusiastic and admiring crowds in the United States and, eventually, in Europe. That first tour earned $20,000. By 1878, the Jubilee Singers had raised $150,000 for Fisk.

Fisk continued to struggle financially in the 1870s and 1880s even as it turned out a new generation of black leaders. W. E. B. DuBois, who would become the school's most famous graduate, found the curriculum limited but excellent. But what struck him most forcibly when he arrived at Fisk from western Massachusetts in the autumn of 1885 was the richness and variety of the students themselves.

Du Bois carried away a lasting impression of "Pop" Miller, an older student, a former slave whose wife took in washing to keep him in school. The pious Miller once severely rebuked DuBois for dancing. There were sons of field hands and mulatto sons of rich white planters. Fisk admitted women, too, among them the strikingly beautiful Lena Calhoun, great-aunt of the someday-to-be-famous singer Lena Horne.

And, recalled DuBois, "There was black, coarse-looking Sherrod, poor and slow, who worked his way painfully through college, studied medicine at neighboring Meharry Medical School, and became one of the best physicians in Mississippi."[19] ◆

Radical administrations. In Mississippi, the downturn forced Governor Ames to push for spending cuts and tax reductions at the same time the black voters who had put him in power were calling for increases in state aid for schools and other social programs. Ames also vetoed a bill that declared a stay in debt collection and repealed the crop lien law that allowed creditors first claim on a farmer's harvest. Though these measures had widespread support among blacks, Ames believed they would worsen the effects of the depression by drying up supplies and credit for landowners and tenants alike. The governor also cut spending for higher education, abolished state college scholarships, and reduced the salaries of public officials.

Even with these setbacks, Mississippi could claim political firsts and social gains. In 1872, Lynch won election to Congress and at age 24 became its youngest member. Two years later, Mississippi sent Blanche K. Bruce, born in Virginia of a slave mother in 1841, to the U.S. Senate. Educated at Oberlin College in Ohio and a printer by trade, Bruce came to Mississippi in 1868 and made a small fortune as a cotton planter. He became the first African American to serve a full term in the Senate, where his chief policy interests were Mississippi River improvements and fairer policies toward Indians.

The state's Republicans could claim enduring successes in a number of areas. As in South Carolina and other states, Republicans established a school system—primitive, though far in advance of anything the state had known before. They supported teacher training institutes and, in 1871, founded Alcorn University, a state university for blacks. They reformed the state judiciary, adopted a new legal code that struck discriminatory laws off the books, founded state hospitals, and improved asylums for the blind, deaf, and insane. In 1873, the legislature approved a civil rights bill that, in theory at least, granted blacks equal access to public places.

Republican government in Mississippi owed its success in no small measure to the contributions of the rising class of black public officials. Concluded historian Vernon Wharton: "With their white Republican colleagues, they gave to the state a government of greatly expanded functions, at a cost that was low in comparison with that of almost any other state."[16] To intransigent whites, that was beside the point. They refused to countenance any black participation in public life. By the summer of 1874, a "White Man's Party" in Vicksburg had begun experimenting with an arsenal of violent political tactics that would be employed to the maximum in a murderous effort to "redeem" Mississippi from Republican rule.

NOTES

1. Eric Foner, *Reconstruction: America's Unfinished Revolution, 1863–1877* (New York: Harper & Row, 1988), 320–21.

2. Foner, *Reconstruction*, 348.

3. First quote, Kenneth M. Stampp, *The Era of Reconstruction; 1865–1877* (New York: Alfred A. Knopf, 1965), 168; second quote, Elizabeth Ware Pearson, ed., *Letters from Port Royal, 1862–1868* (New York: Arno Press, 1969 reprint edition), 328.

4. Foner, *Reconstruction*, 350.

5. First quote, Foner, *Reconstruction*, 361; second quote, Virginia Writers' Program, *The Negro in Virginia* (New York: Arno Press, 1969, reprint), 229.

6. W. E. B. DuBois, *Black Reconstruction in America* (New York: Russell & Russell, 1962), 408.

7. First quote, Foner, *Reconstruction*, 369; second quote, Stampp, *The Era of Reconstruction*, 169; third quote, Foner, *Reconstruction*, 298.

8. Foner, *Reconstruction*, 363.

9. Foner, *Reconstruction*, 405, 409.

10. Foner, *Reconstruction*, 408, 409.

11. DuBois, *Black Reconstruction*, 428.

12. Foner, *Reconstruction*, 385.

13. Richard W. Murphy, *The Nation Reunited: War's Aftermath* (Alexandria, Va.: Time-Life Books, 1987), 106, 108.

14. First quote, Foner, *Reconstruction*, 387; second quote, DuBois, *Black Reconstruction*, 402; third quote, Foner, *Reconstruction*, 388.

15. Foner, *Reconstruction*, 296.

16. Vernon L. Wharton, *The Negro in Mississippi, 1865–1900* (New York: Harper & Row, 1965), 180.

17. John W. Blassingame, ed., *Slave Testimony* (Baton Rouge: Louisiana State University Press, 1977), 620.

18. Blassingame, ed., *Slave Testimony*, 620.

19. W. E. B. DuBois, *The Autobiography of W. E. B. DuBois* (New York: International Publishers, 1968).

7

Reaction and "Redemption": 1870–1877

$\mathbf{V}$iolence had long been a way of life in the South. In the pre–Civil War era, whites of the planter class—they thought of themselves as "cava-liers"—reached instinctively for their weapons as a means of settling a quarrel. In an infamous example, the South Caro-lina congressman Preston Brooks caned abolitionist senator Charles Sumner nearly to death at the Capitol in Washington in 1856. Slaveholders were notorious for their reliance on the whip to punish disobedient slaves. After the war, guns and knives were everywhere. "Could you brush against any

Currier & Ives published this lithograph of black members of the U.S. Congress in 1872. Seated, from left: Senator Hiram Revels of Mississippi and Representatives Benjamin S. Turner of Alabama, Josiah T. Walls of Florida, Joseph H. Rainey of South Carolina, and Robert Brown Elliott of South Carolina. Standing: Robert L. De Large of South Carolina, left, and Jefferson H. Long of Georgia. (New York Public Library, Schomburg Center for Research in Black Culture)

ragged neighbor without being bruised by his concealed weapon?" Whitelaw Reid wondered.[1] In this context, white conservatives' increasing use of terror to achieve the overthrow of black-supported Reconstruction governments—what whites called Redemption—seemed entirely in keeping with Southern practice.

Wary of federal power, the opposition Democrats moved cautiously at first. The "New Departure" political movement did not directly challenge black suffrage, choosing to focus instead on taxation and spending issues and the restoration of voting rights to former Confederates. In Alabama in 1870, Robert Lindsay, the Democratic candidate for governor, actively courted African-American support. In any case, whites could use more subtle means to lessen the impact of black political activity. "It don't matter how the people vote as long as we count the ballots," one Democrat remarked.[2]

Opposition parties elsewhere made efforts to attract black votes, though rarely out of any regard for the democratic process. "We are led to this course not through choice, but by necessity—by the stern logic of events," a Mississippi newspaper commented in 1871.[3] Democratic candidates in Louisiana and Georgia also backed off the race issue temporarily. In Georgia, Democrats captured the state legislature in 1870 and the governorship the following year. The "Redeemer" governor, James M. Smith, promptly advised blacks to forget about politics and "get down to honest hard work." Georgia's legislature imposed a poll tax and enacted strict residency and registration requirements in an effort to reduce the black vote.

When peaceful means didn't work, whites turned to intimidation and violence to drive blacks from political life. Former Confederate soldiers formed secret white supremacist organizations such as the Ku Klux Klan that used paramilitary tactics to carry out beatings, whippings, and murders on an unprecedented scale. They burned black schools, churches and homes. They destroyed black farmers' crops and livestock. In an incident that could be multiplied a thousandfold in the postwar South, a gang of Chattanooga whites severely beat a black politician named Andrew Flowers shortly after he had the misfortune to win a local election as a justice of the peace. Recalled Flowers afterward: "They said they had nothing in particular against me, that they didn't dispute I was a very good fellow, but they did not intend any nigger to hold office in the United States."[4]

There were attacks on African Americans' white allies as well. Georgia Klansmen murdered three scalawag members of the state legislature. Klan thugs in North Carolina assassinated a Republican state senator. White supremacists whipped a North Carolina planter who had distributed land to his former slaves. Armed whites broke up a black political meeting in Greene County, Alabama, killing four blacks and wounding more than 50. In Laurens County, South Carolina, 13 freedmen were murdered the day after an election in which the Republicans were victorious.

For a time, the Klan operated unchecked. Federal authorities lacked the resources to crush the white terror organizations. Most of the U.S. troops had been withdrawn. By 1869, only 716 bluecoats remained in Mississippi. Blacks tried to fight back. In some South Carolina towns, armed freedmen patrolled the streets at night. Generally, though, they found themselves outgunned: their shotguns and black-powder pistols were no match for the modern repeating rifles and six-chamber revolvers with which their tormentors, usually battle-tested former Confederate soldiers, were armed.

Escalating Klan violence finally pushed Congress to pass a series of Enforcement Acts in 1870–71. The acts made it a federal crime to deprive citizens of the right to vote, hold office, serve on juries, and enjoy equal protection of the law. A federal crackdown in 1871 led to a sharp, though temporary, decrease in the level of violence. Thousands of KKK suspects were indicted. With a declaration of martial law in nine counties of upcountry South Carolina, as many as 2,000 Klansmen fled the state. Few of those indicted went to jail, however. Most received suspended sentences; many escaped punishment entirely.

A rigid political dividing line—blacks to the Republican party, whites to the Democrats—evolved out of the inexorable logic of Southern racial antagonism. African Americans had a saying that became an article of faith: "The Republican Party is the boat and all else but the empty sea."[5] Scalawags and, eventually, carpetbaggers too—at least those who chose to settle permanently in the states of the old Confederacy—went over in increasing numbers into the Democratic Party. For many, the choice became an imperative. Colonel James Lusk, a former Confederate officer and a leading

Mississippi Republican, allied himself with the Democrats reluctantly, but permanently. Lusk explained the realities to a black Republican ally, Sam Henry:

> No white man can live in the South in the future and act with any other than the Democratic party unless he is willing and prepared to live a life of social isolation and political oblivion. Besides, I have two grown sons. There is, no doubt, a bright, brilliant and successful future before them if they are Democrats, otherwise not. Then, you must remember that a man's first duty is to his family. My daughters are the pride of my home. I cannot afford to have them suffer the humiliating consequences of the social ostracism to which they may be subjected if I remain in the Republican party.[6]

White resistance did not cease with the "redemption" of most of the South. In 1874, four states remained under multiracial Republican government: Louisiana, Mississippi, Florida, and South Carolina. The familiar patterns of violence and intimidation were soon restored in those states, against a backdrop of growing indifference in the North. Part of the explanation lay in the long depression that followed the Panic of 1873. People's concerns were close to home: their jobs, their future. Politicians understood this, and Reconstruction slipped far down on the list of national priorities. Some saw a deeper underlying cause for the waning of Northern support for the surviving Radical governments. Amos Akerman, who as President Grant's attorney general had ultimate responsibility for enforcing federal law in the South, offered this explanation: "The Northern mind, being active, and full of what is called progress, runs away from the past. Even such atrocities as Ku Kluxery do not hold their attention."[7] Carl Schurz, E. L. Godkin, and many other one-time Radicals lost interest in the troubles of the freed

This Democratic campaign badge of 1868 stirred racial animosity in the North. (New York Public Library, Schomburg Center for Research in Black Culture)

people, directing their energies instead to such issues as civil service reform.

Southern Democrats were quick to sense and exploit the shift. "You might as well quit," a Democrat warned a black Republican campaign worker in 1874. "We will carry the state or kill half of you on election day." As it happened, levels of violence in Alabama were modest compared with those in neighboring Mississippi. The "Mississippi Plan," as it became known, served as a euphemism for political terror of the grossest and most unrestrained sort. "Mississippi is a white man's country, and by the Eternal God we'll rule it," the *Yazoo City Banner* declared.[8] Democrats formed irregular militia units, disrupted Republican meetings, marched heavily armed through black communities, provoked riots, carried out execution-style murders, and posted armed detachments at polling places to keep blacks from voting.

White-liners (white supremacists) first tried out elements of the Mississippi Plan in Vicksburg in the summer of 1874. A "White Man's Party" sent armed groups out to patrol the streets of the old river town. During the campaign, whites vowed to use every means, not excluding homicide, to suppress the black vote. Adelbert Ames, the state's carpetbagger governor, found himself powerless to quell the uprising. President Grant turned down Ames's requests for assistance, establishing a pattern of federal indifference that would persist until Reconstruction met its final, violent end.

"I have tried to get troops, but the President refuses," a dejected Ames wrote his wife on August 2, 1874. "They in Vicksburg who are rioting, who are ready for murder and frauds, laud him to the skies."[9] Ames had only one company of militia in Vicksburg on which he felt he could rely. But they were black troops, and Ames feared that calling them out would touch off an orgy of racial killing. He did not even bother to issue any orders to the state's white militia companies, assuming that they would ignore them anyway.

Whites swept the Vicksburg elections and took control of the city. That turned out to be only the beginning, in Mississippi and elsewhere. In the 1874 mid-term national elections, the Democrats regained control of Congress, signaling a further retreat from Reconstruction. "What a revolution!" Ames wrote. "In fact, I hardly realize it. A Democratic Congress! And the war not yet over."[10] Democratic successes in the North emboldened Mississippi whites. In Jackson, the state capital, wrote Ames's wife Blanche, the crack of the pistol had become as frequent as the barking of dogs.

Vicksburg became the flashpoint for white revolt. In December 1874, heavily armed White-liners demanded the resignation of the black Republican sheriff, Peter Crosby. Crosby fled to Jackson for protection. On the morning of December 7, a group of country blacks marched into Vicksburg in support of Crosby. A party of some 80 white vigilantes met the marchers in the courthouse square. Few of the blacks were armed; none made any attempt to use a weapon. Nevertheless, the white mob opened fire into the crowd, killing at least 29. In the aftermath, White-liners roved the countryside about Vicksburg. As many as 300 blacks were murdered.

Again, Ames lacked the strength to restore order in Vicksburg and its hinterland. He again asked Grant for federal assistance. "A portion of our territory is under control of insurgents," Ames wrote the president. "I have not the power to suppress an insurrection."[11] In early January Grant finally acted, ordering a company of regular troops to Jackson. Ames had the impression—a false one, as it turned out—that Grant would send reinforcements if necessary.

By the election season of 1875, the Mississippi Plan had been fully tested. The *Hinds County Gazette* put the matter bluntly:

> All other means having been exhausted to abate the horrible condition of things, the thieves and robbers,

and scoundrels, white and black, deserve death and ought to be killed. Carry the election peaceably if we can, forcibly if we must.[12]

The 1875 Democratic platform acknowledged black civil and political rights, but it was clearly a dead letter. The *Meridian Mercury* spoke openly of the eventual goal of redemption of all the South from Republican rule: "The Negro, in these states, will be a slave again or cease to be. His sole refuge from extinction will be in slavery to the white man."[13] So the campaign began. Blacks lost their jobs for voting Republican. No man who supported the Republicans could expect a labor contract for the following year. Doctors announced that they would refuse to treat anyone who collaborated with the common political enemy.

These measures were mild in comparison with what followed. When African Americans persisted in expressing their political preferences, whites turned violent. Democratic rifle clubs broke up black political meetings. Taking advantage of Governor Ames's indecisiveness and his fear of a race war, they made little effort to disguise their activities, carrying out many of their operations in broad daylight. In Yazoo County on September 1, 1875, a white militia company attacked blacks at a Republican rally. Several black politicians, including a state legislator, were murdered. A few days later, another group broke up a black political barbecue near Jackson, killing several. Afterwards, the white mob roamed the countryside. The death toll reached 30. Former governor James Alcorn, the one-time scalawag, formed his own gang. In one of their first efforts, Alcorn's roughs broke up a Coahoma County meeting, adding more names to the death toll.

In Vicksburg, black citizens petitioned Ames for protection. "They are going around the streets at night dressed in soldiers' clothes and making the colored people run for their lives," the appeal read. "We will not vote at all, unless there are troops to protect us." On September 7, Ames issued a proclamation ordering the white militias to disband. They ignored the order. "Ha! Ha!! Ha!!!," the *Jackson Clarion* jeered. "'Command. Disband.' That's good."[14] In many districts, blacks, fearing for their lives, dropped out of politics altogether.

Ames renewed his appeals to Grant. The president more or less delegated the matter to Edward Pierrepont, who had succeeded Akerman as attorney general. Pierrepont had no sympathy for Ames's troubles. Besides, he worried about political effects. "The whole public are tired out with these autumnal outbreaks in the South," Pierrepont said.[15] Ames, rightly, took Pierrepont's dismissive remark to mean that the Grant Administration would take no further action in the matter.

With Pierrepont's assistance, Ames and the insurgent Democrats worked out an agreement that purported to promise a truce and a peaceful election. Ames agreed to disband the only two companies of militia available to him in return for a Democratic promise to disarm. The Democrats, it turned out, did not even bother to pretend to carry out the terms of the accord.

"It was the most violent time that we have ever seen," one black officeholder lamented.[16] The rampages continued through Election Day. In Aberdeen, in an incident that could stand as the classic expression of the Mississippi Plan, whites used a six-pounder cannon and a detachment of cavalry to keep blacks from the polls. The result was a complete Democratic success. In 1873, Ames had carried Yazoo County, with an overwhelming black majority, by 1,800 votes. Two years later, Democrats polled 4,044 votes—to *seven* for the Republicans. Democrats took five of six congressional seats (only John Lynch survived the deluge) and four out of every five seats in the state legislature.

"Yes," an utterly defeated Governor Ames wrote his wife, "a *revolution* has taken place—by force of arms—and a race disenfranchised—they are to be returned to a condition of serfdom—an era of second slavery."[17]

The final acts were swift and brutal. Majority Democrats impeached the black lieutenant governor, Alexander Davis, and drove him from office. Then, in March 1876, they brought impeachment articles against Ames himself. The Democrats accused the governor of inciting the Vicksburg riots, appointing incompetents to state posts, and accepting bribes. The charges were outrageous, but Ames had lost all heart to fight them. He worked out a deal: He would resign and leave the state in return for the dropping of the charges. Ames eventually went into the flour-milling business in Minnesota. Within a year, the Mississippi Republican Executive Committee adopted a resolution formally dissolving the party in the state.

Politics were almost as hazardous in South Carolina, Florida, and Louisiana. By mid-1874, some 14,000 White Leaguers had turned Louisiana into a racial battleground. To control them, Republican governor William P. Kellogg could call on a token garrison of 130 U.S. troops. Grant ignored his pleas for more help. A small army of 3,500 White Leaguers, most of them Confederate veterans, routed a detachment of black militia and New Orleans police under the command of former Confederate general James Longstreet and forced the Kellogg government to flee. Grant acted at last, sending troops to restore Kellogg to his rightful office. The mobs remained defiant. "The White League is the only power in the state," one mob leader boasted.[18]

Southern whites took heart from the absence of a Northern response to the war against the freed people. By the mid-1870s, the period of congressional activism had all but passed. In 1872, Congress passed an Amnesty Act restoring full political rights to nearly all former Confederates. Three years later, Congress made its last feeble attempt to provide legal protection for former slaves, approving the Civil Rights Act of 1875. This was meant to guarantee civil and political rights and to prohibit social segregation in public places. Violators were subject to fines and jail terms. Few efforts were made, however, to enforce the law.

In any case, the U.S. Supreme Court, in a series of rulings, undermined much of what Congress had sought to achieve. In 1873, the decisions known collectively as the "Slaughterhouse Cases" effectively denied blacks the use of the federal courts to seek redress against oppressive state laws. In 1875, the high court ruled that the Constitution "does not confer the right of suffrage upon anyone." (This case specifically turned on the question of women's suffrage, but it affected African Americans equally.) The court also voided sections of the Ku Klux Klan enforcement laws. Finally, in 1883, the Supreme Court struck down the 1875 Civil Rights Act.

By 1876, only Louisiana, Florida, and South Carolina remained under Radical rule. For whites intent on regaining power, South Carolina posed perhaps the most difficult test. Whites formed only about 40 percent of the electorate there. Even so, white Carolinians were united—only 3,000 or so were estimated to consistently vote Republican—and they had an effective leader in Wade Hampton, scion of an old South Carolina family, prewar owner of hundreds of slaves and a Confederate cavalry commander with a distinguished fighting record in the Civil War.

Hampton had been out of the state during long stretches in the early 1870s, rebuilding his fortune on the family cottonlands in Mississippi. He did, however, exert considerable influence in a quiet way. In public, the patrician Hampton appeared to be a model of moderation. Privately, Hampton denounced emancipation, which had nearly ruined him financially, derided the Freedmen's Bureau, and advocated the expulsion of blacks from the United States. He also headed a legal defense fund for accused South Carolina Klansmen.

Hampton became known as a "cooperationist"—a Democrat willing to allow blacks some political rights. He and his allies made efforts to attract black votes. At first, these efforts

For some blacks, the U.S. Army offered escape from the tensions of post–Civil War Southern life. Four regular regiments of black troops—the famous Buffalo Soldiers—served in the postwar U.S. Army, mostly on the western frontier. These soldiers are on duty as stagecoach escorts, doubtless to guard the bags of valuables on the ground near the vehicle. (National Archives)

were almost comically inept. At campaign rallies in the early 1870s, Democrats set up two separate platforms—one for whites, the other for blacks. Few freedmen showed any taste for the Democratic campaign style. Democrats advanced the argument that the leaders of the South Carolina planter class were blacks' "true friends"; that native blacks and whites had grown up together; that Republican carpetbaggers were interested in blacks only as a means to power. Hardly any African Americans were persuaded. "We have played together, you say," a Republican campaign streamer read, "but were we ever whipped together?" Hampton let it be known that he had no objection to blacks serving in Congress (Robert Smalls remained unassailable in his Sea Islands bastion), so long as "they will let us have the state."[19] He and his followers resolved to take it, by fair means or foul.

The 1876 Democratic ticket consisted wholly of former Confederate officers, Hampton and the others campaigning on the issues of heavy taxation, extravagant state spending, and public corruption. Hampton sought black votes; though he offered no specific policies of interest to blacks, he did promise "free men, free schools, free votes." And he called, eloquently and with evident sincerity, for racial peace.

Unlike most Democratic politicians of the era, Hampton inspired a certain amount of trust among blacks. "General Hampton could not tell a lie," a black Democrat named Robinson told a political rally. The candidate, Robinson went on, had assured him "he would give his people good teachers both male and female, and that he would keep the school house open more than four months a year."[20] Still, most blacks doubted that Hampton would be able to deliver on his pledges, even if he wanted to do so. In any case, in upcountry South Carolina, where the white and black populations were more nearly equal in number, Democrats made far greater efforts at suppression than at persuasion.

Democrats crisscrossed the state to mobilize the white vote. Hampton traveled with an an escort of hundreds of armed and mounted supporters—the famous "Red Shirts," a color chosen deliberately to suggest blood. This political cavalry drew large crowds of whites. From time to time, the Democrats would bring in a few cooperative blacks, to give the illusion that they were running an open campaign. At a gathering in Edgefield, a reporter counted nine blacks in a crowd of 1,600 Hampton horsemen.

Hampton may have forsworn violence, but his supporters did no such thing. Inspired by the Mississippi redemption of the year before, Democratic rifle clubs broke up Republican political meetings, whipped freedmen in public, and carried out political murders and arsons. For a change, black Republicans not only fought back but in some cases went on the offensive. Hampton's few black supporters—they included the former Freedmen's Bureau functionary Martin Delany—were harassed and, on several occasions, beaten. A party of blacks opened fire on a political meeting in Cainhoy near Charleston, killing five whites and one black Democrat.

As before, President Grant did nothing to ensure a fair election. And as always, Democrats had the edge on their opponents in discipline, organization, and firepower. On Election Day in Edgefield, Democrats removed the ballot box from the portico of the courthouse to a room inside. Armed whites filled the building and several hundred horsemen surrounded it. "Not more than 35 or 40 Colard men voted at this box during the entire day," one black political leader reported.[21] Hundreds either stayed away or were turned away from the polling station.

Such tactics, repeated elsewhere in South Carolina, brought the Democrats a narrow victory. Thousands of blacks were prevented from reaching the polls, and Hampton eventually won the disputed election by around a thousand votes. The Republicans did not give up easily, however. They challenged the result, and for a period of four months a dual government ruled the state—Hampton claiming the governorship, the apparently defeated Republican incumbent, Daniel Chamberlain, refusing to yield it.

In the presidential election of 1876, Republican candidate Rutherford B. Hayes emerged with what appeared to be a one-vote Electoral College victory over Democrat Samuel Tilden, even though Tilden actually won the popular vote. The ambiguous result set off a winter-long political crisis. Republican election boards in the disputed states of South Carolina, Florida, and Louisiana invalidated enough Democratic ballots to keep their states nominally Republican and deliver their electoral votes to Hayes. Democrats challenged the Republican actions.

In South Carolina, federal troops surrounded the statehouse in Columbia, keeping Hampton out. In the North,

Rise and Fall of a Black Carpetbagger

The remarkable career of black carpetbagger Robert Brown Elliott ran in exact parallel with the history of Radical Reconstruction. He rose as though on wings to the upper reaches of political power. His fall, when it came, was sudden, hard, and conclusive.

Elliott made a great mystery of his background and seems to have fabricated much of it. He claimed to have been born in Boston in 1842 of West Indian parents and educated there and in England. More likely he was English-born. He probably reached Boston early in 1867 as a deserter from a Royal Navy warship.

At any rate, Elliott turned up later in 1867 in Charleston, South Carolina, where he became an editor of a Republican newspaper called the *South Carolina Leader*. In 1868 he won election to the state constitutional convention and claimed a seat in the state House of Representatives. At the same time, he read enough law to gain admission to the South Carolina bar. In 1870 he won the first of two terms in the U.S. Congress.

Elliott built a strong constituency among the freed people. A blunt and forceful advocate for his race, he urged blacks to demand their rights and to refuse to accept second-class treatment. He also campaigned, successfully, for a larger share of political offices for African Americans. This

Hayes's operatives worked furiously to strike a deal that would break the deadlock. Southern representatives in Congress insisted on Home Rule—meaning exclusive white rule—in return for a settlement that would give Hayes the White House.

The details of the agreement that made Hayes president remain murky. Whatever it involved, it enabled the Democrats to complete the "redemption" of the South. On April 10, 1877, President Hayes ordered federal troops out of the earned him the fear and hatred of many whites. A reporter for *The New York Times*, observing the mixed respect and dread that Elliott seemed to inspire, described him as "very black, very well spoken and bitter as gall."[24]

As a state legislator, he argued for a law banning discrimination in public places; in Congress he spoke out for federal suppression of the Ku Klux Klan and against a political amnesty measure for former Confederates. Always, in whatever role, Elliott made a point of puncturing white pretensions to supremacy. During the Klan outrages of 1869–71, he framed a simple question to demolish the white argument that blacks were not civilized enough to govern. "Pray tell me," he asked, alluding to the Klan, "who is the barbarian here?"[25]

Elliott tried and failed to move up to the Senate in 1872. In a corrupt contest, his opponent handed out bribes liberally to buy support; Elliott turned down $15,000 to drop out of the race. He resigned from Congress in 1874 to return to the South Carolina legislature, where he served as Speaker of the House until 1876.

Elected attorney general of South Carolina during the disputed election of 1876, Elliott was forced from office when the Democrats returned to power. This was the effective end of his political career. In debt and ailing, he moved to New Orleans, where he held a minor patronage job as a U.S. treasury agent.

He died of malarial fever in New Orleans in 1884. Only 42 years old, Elliott had packed a lifetime's political experience into eight brilliant years. ◆

South Carolina capitol, allowing Hampton to take power. Two weeks later, the U.S. garrison withdrew from the statehouse in Baton Rouge, giving the Democrats control of Louisiana's government.

The experiment of Reconstruction thus came to a close. "The whole South—every state in the South—had got into the hands of the very men that held us as slaves," Louisianan Henry Adams noted in a somber assessment. "The negro will disappear from the field of national politics," *The Nation* announced. "Henceforth, the nation, as a nation, will have nothing more to do with him."[22] So it was. Hayes pursued what he dubbed a "let alone" policy toward the South. The effect was to confirm a white rule that became increasingly absolute. Blacks were pushed to the political margins. Within a decade or so, the long night of Jim Crow would descend in every state of the old Confederacy.

The triumph of the white conservatives failed, however, to bring peace to the tortured South. Blacks refused to let go of their dreams of educational and economic opportunity, civil rights, and political power.

In an 1875 speech urging Congress to pass the Civil Rights Act, black South Carolina representative R. H. Cain had issued a warning. "You sought to make the reconstruction acts a nullity," he said, directing his remarks specifically to white Southerners. "You sought to re-enslave the black man by every means in your power. It is because you refused to accept the situation that there is now strife in the land. And I will tell you further that there will be strife all over this land as long as the rights of any class of men are trampled underfoot, North, South, East or West."[23]

NOTES

1. Whitelaw Reid, *After the War: A Tour of the Southern States, 1865–1866*, C. Vann Woodward, ed. (New York: Harper & Row, 1965), 422.

2. Rembert W. Patrick, *Reconstruction of the Nation* (New York: Oxford University Press, 1967), 252.

3. Eric Foner, *Reconstruction: America's Unfinished Revolution, 1863–1877* (New York: Harper & Row, 1988), 417.

4. Foner, *Reconstruction*, 427.

5. Virginia Writers' Program, *The Negro in Virginia* (New York: Arno Press, 1969 reprint), 233.

6. John Roy Lynch, *Reminiscences of an Active Life*, John Hope Franklin, ed. (Chicago: University of Chicago Press, 1970), 151.

7. Richard W. Murphy, *The Nation Reunited: War's Aftermath* (Alexandria, Va.: Time-Life Books, 1987), 97.

8. First quote, Murphy, *Nation Reunited*, 145; second quote, Vernon L. Wharton, *The Negro in Mississippi, 1865–1900* (New York: Harper & Row, 1965), 184.

9. Blanche A. Ames, *Adelbert Ames, 1835–1933: General, Senator, Governor* (New York: Antiquarian Press, 1964), 396.

10. Ames, *Adelbert Ames*, 402.

11. Ames, *Adelbert Ames*, 413.

12. Kenneth M. Stampp, *The Era of Reconstruction, 1865–1877* (New York: Alfred A. Knopf, 1965), 201.

13. Murphy, *Nation Reunited*, 148.

14. Wharton, *The Negro in Mississippi*, 193.

15. Ames, *Adelbert Ames*, 430.

16. Foner, *Reconstruction*, 561.

17. Ames, *Adelbert Ames*, 434.

18. Murphy, *Nation Reunited*, 143.

19. First quote, Joel Williamson, *After Slavery: The Negro in South Carolina during Reconstruction, 1861–1877* (Chapel Hill: University of North Carolina Press, 1965), 395; second quote, Foner, *Reconstruction*, 574.

20. Williamson, *After Slavery*, 428.

21. Williamson, *After Slavery*, 345.

22. Foner, *Reconstruction*, 582 (both quotes).

23. Leslie Fishel, Jr., and Benjamin Quarles, *The Black American: A Documentary History* (New York: William Morrow & Company, 1970), 285.

24. Leon Litwack and August Meier, ed., *Black Leaders of the Nineteeth Century* (Urbana: University of Illinois Press, 1988), 202.

25. Foner, *Reconstruction*, 443.

8

The New South: 1877–1905

The white conservative Redeemers who forced their way into power in the South in the 1870s exaggerated, for political purposes, the number of blacks in public office during Reconstruction. In his book *The Prostrate State* (1873), Northern journalist James S. Pike wrote luridly of the excesses and inefficiencies of black politicians. In fact, as has been noted, Radical Republicans, black and white, gave South Carolina perhaps the best state government it had ever known. Still, the reports of Pike and others gave the impression that gangs of corrupt, illiterate field hands had ruled the South.

In fact, Radical officeholders, black and white, performed at least as well (and as honestly) as any other group and often better. Blacks actually held only a few major offices, even during the full flood of Radical rule. Blacks won no governorships during Reconstruction, though there were a number of black lieutenant governors and other senior state officials. Fourteen African Americans served in the U.S. House of Representatives; two African Americans were elected to the U.S. Senate, both from Mississippi. Only in South Carolina did blacks ever enjoy a majority in a state legislature.

With the withdrawal of the last of the federal garrisons, resurgent conservatives moved to consolidate their political power. Of course, blacks did not cease to vote all at once, and some Redeemer leaders swore for several years after 1876 that black disenfranchisement was not their goal. Even so, the vehicle for black political expression—the Republican Party—seemed to have broken down irreparably. By 1878 the Democrats had so thoroughly captured South Carolina that the Republicans failed to field a candidate against the incumbent governor, Wade Hampton. In Mississippi, the number of black voters declined precipitously. In Amite County, for example, 1,093 blacks voted in 1873. In 1876, a year after the Democrats returned to power, 73 blacks voted in the county.

Despite the setbacks, an aging Frederick Douglass continued to labor on behalf of the freed people. "Bulldozing and Kukluxing, Mississippi plans, fraudulent counts, tissue ballots and the like devices," he told a political convention in Louisville in the early 1880s, had muffled the political voice of Southern blacks. "The colored citizens of those states are virtually disenfranchised, the Constitution held in utter contempt and its provisions nullified."[1] But blacks' former Northern allies were no longer listening.

The victory of the white conservatives was so complete that they had little need for serious reprisal. In South Carolina, Democrats made some effort to bring allegedly corrupt officials to trial. James Connor, Hampton's attorney general, seemed less concerned about whether evidence of corruption would meet legal tests than about the moral effect of indictments. "The press would revel in it," Connor wrote an associate, "& we would politically guillotine every man of them."[2] Even in South Carolina, "the prostrate state," Democrats found it imprudent to push corruption investigations far. Too many of their own people had been involved.

African Americans continued to hold local offices and serve in state legislatures well into the 1880s. Robert Smalls, the Sea Islands political boss, won election to Congress as late as 1884. John Lynch persisted in running for Congress from a largely black district in Mississippi. As time went on, though, fraud and intimidation drove all but the most determined blacks out of the political process. In January 1888, only one black citizen of the Mississippi capital even tried to vote. "He was an old negro and looked silly, and he was not hurt, but told to hustle out in double-quick time," the *Jackson New Mississippian* reported.[3]

In state after state, Redeemer governments cut spending and enacted regressive tax laws. The new tax systems tended to shift the burden from large landowners to small farmers, tenant farmers, and artisans. Tools were heavily taxed, for example. "The farmer's hoe and plow, and the mechanic's saw and plane, must be taxed to support the government," a Georgia newspaper complained. "Show me the rich man who handles a hoe or pushes a plane."[4] Many Democrats saw education, especially black education, as a luxury their states could not afford. Texas began charging fees for schooling. In Florida, the legislature shut down the state's agricultural college. Per capita spending for black schools in South Carolina fell by more than half from 1880 to 1895, in spite of Hampton's campaign promises.

So the bright hopes of the early years of emancipation faded with the passing years. Rufus Saxton, the Yankee general associated with the government's abortive land distribution program of 1865, admitted as much in a letter to Robert Smalls that recalled emancipation ceremonies in Beaufort on January

1, 1863. "Never in all his round did a glad sun shine upon a scene of more dramatic power," Saxton wrote. "What a day of promise that was!"[5] He did not need to add that, in much of the South, the promise had not been fulfilled.

The agricultural depression of the 1870s prolonged hard times in the South, which had barely begun to recover from wartime damage and the social dislocations of emancipation before the bottom dropped out of cotton prices. As cotton production gradually climbed—it finally reached prewar levels in the South as a whole in 1878—prices fell. By 1878 cotton was bringing only eight cents a pound, down from 12 cents eight years earlier. Production of Sea Island cotton, much sought-after in prewar days, continued to lag. Impoverished white islanders could not afford to work large acreages, and black smallholders remained content to grow food crops, raising only modest amounts of cotton for "cash money."

Many Port Royal blacks did manage to hold onto their small plots of land. Elsewhere, sharecropping and tenant farming were the norm. Thousands of African Americans continued to work as farmhands, without such economic opportunity as even sharecropping could provide. These conditions perpetuated the cycle of poverty and debt. A contract between an Adams County, Mississippi planter and a black farm laborer gives an idea of the terms of work in the 1880s:

> John Warren agrees to work ten (10) months of 26 working days to a month he to do all kinds of work such as plowing hoeing chopping work & such as is done about farming and about a house he is to work honestly the hours usually worked by such help. P. Murphy to pay him 4 dollars cash per month as above and 4 dollars more the first of January 1886 to give him a room & a little spot for a garden rent free, while working for P. Murphy also for *each week* he *works* to give him 5 lbs of Pork one peck of corn meal ½ lb of coffee and one lb of sugar.

Murphy also stipulated that Warren would forfeit any pay due him if he left before the expiration of the contract or if he stole. "I want it plainley understood that there is to be *no stealing* or taking anything without permission," Murphy insisted.[6] Warren endorsed the agreement with "his X mark."

The planter class suffered too. It became increasingly difficult to coax a livelihood out of the land, hardly worthwhile to take the trouble to exploit one's tenants or laborers. "He can not get much advantage of his laborers, because they are already at *hardpan*," an agricultural expert remarked of the 1880s Georgia planter. "He can not make much by dealing unfairly with them."[7] In 1880, the South's per capita income stood at only 40 percent of the North's.

In several states, Democratic legislatures drafted laws to give planters maximum control over the labor force. In some states it became a criminal offense to walk off a job before the expiration of a contract. In North Carolina, a Landlord and Tenant Act allowed a planter to hold an entire year's crop until his tenant had paid the rent.

Penal codes were overhauled, nearly always to the detriment of blacks. In South Carolina, a man convicted of burglary could be sentenced to life in prison. Mississippi's infamous "pig law" made theft of any property valued at more than $10, or of any cattle or swine, grand larceny punishable by up to five years in prison. Most states imposed jail terms for petty offenses such as drunkenness and vagrancy. Throughout the South, blacks were far more likely than whites to be arrested for minor infractions. As a result, Southern jails filled up with blacks, a circumstance that gave rise to the notorious convict-lease system.

Under the leasing laws, states or counties would hire out convicts to lumbering companies, mining concerns, railroad builders, and other large businesses. In Mississippi, roughly a thousand convicts, the majority of them African Americans, were leased out for work at any one time, usually at bargain rates. Conditions were brutal—as bad as any to be found at any time in American history. Convict leasing, one investigator concluded, had a parallel only in the persecutions of the Dark Ages. There were elements, too, of what totalitarian states of the 20th century would refine in the form of labor camps. Death rates were appalling, especially for blacks. In one group of 204 convicts leased out for work, 20 were reported to have died and 23 were returned to prison ill or otherwise disabled—all in one six-month period. In South Carolina, death rates were said to reach 50 percent at times.

Not all of the Southern landscape was blighted, however. A black business class of shopkeepers, hoteliers, restaurateurs, barbers, and undertakers began to form in the cities and towns. Black businessmen called on the black community for support. "We cannot write any white insurance business and the white agent is controlling the insurance situation in our homes," ran one such appeal. "This will never do! Break it up! Get the business."[8] Ironically, the gradual imposition of strict racial segregation encouraged the development of black-owned businesses.

Fisk, Howard, and other black colleges that had been established during Reconstruction managed to survive, even to prosper. Mississippi Democrats reduced funding for Alcorn University, but the school grew modestly anyway during the 1880s.

A substantial number of rural blacks managed, against the odds, to acquire their own farms in the last decades of the century. By 1900, according to one study, close to a quarter of all black farmers owned the land they worked. The farms were small, though, and proportions of black ownership were lowest in the Georgia-Alabama-Mississippi Black Belt, the region with the highest concentration of black population. In the poorer country districts of the Upper South, small farmers were fortunate to make a bare subsistence. A sympathetic white observer described the painstaking process of material accumulation among blacks in the rural South:

First a cow was bought, then an old horse or a lame mule. Now they have as substantial vehicles and as good animals as their old white masters. In their houses, too, they have beds instead of bunks, varnished tables, painted chairs. Many have sewing machines; a few have a piano or an organ.[9]

New opportunities arose in the Mississippi Delta country in the 1880s, where expansion of the railroads and the completion of river levee systems opened up large tracts of fertile land. Blacks migrated to the Delta in large numbers and many found a measure of success there. "The gin crews and engineers are practically all negroes, and there are negro foremen, agents and sub-managers," wrote white planter Alfred Holt Stone. "There are many constables, and there is in my county a negro justice of the peace. In my own town every mail carrier is a negro, and we have a negro on the police force."[10] For a time, more blacks than whites owned land in the Delta.

In general, though, the 1880s were grim times for the mass of African Americans. "The South is a pretty good organized mob and will remain so until bursted by the federal government," A. N. Jackson, a black Alabama pastor, lamented in 1892.[11] Indeed, conditions grew even worse in the 1890s, especially in the Deep South. "The slave went free," wrote W. E. B. DuBois, surveying the era; "stood a brief moment in the sun; then moved back again toward slavery."[12] States, counties, and towns threw up an almost impenetrable racial barrier. In many localities, a shadow legal structure developed alongside the machinery of the formal judiciary—lynch law. The South saw more than 150 lynchings a year during the 1890s, and seven out of every ten victims were black. Finally, tiring of the perpetration of elaborate election frauds, Southern whites devised supposedly legal means to permanently disenfranchise blacks.

Florida passed the first "Jim Crow" law in 1887 (the term "Jim Crow" has its origins in a minstrel song). In state after state, legislatures wrote segregation laws that affected every aspect of Southern life. Most of the laws incorporated features of the Black Codes of 1865 and even of the earlier slave codes. Schools and churches had long been separate, sometimes at the insistence of African Americans themselves. Now hospitals, prisons, hotels, restaurants, streetcars, parks, drinking fountains, and courthouse square benches were segregated. Doctors and dentists furnished separate waiting rooms for white and black patients. The city of Atlanta mandated separate elevators for blacks and whites. The city of Jackson, Mississippi ordered all black corpses to be buried in a new blacks-only municipal cemetery.

Railroad segregation laws were enacted in nine Southern states between 1887 and 1891. "One is thrown in much closer communication in the car with one's traveling companions than in the theatre or restaurant," a New Orleans newspaper noted primly, arguing for complete separation of the races.[13] So blacks were made to ride in inferior cars on trains and to sit in segregated waiting rooms in stations. Many blacks protested, and there were many scenes—sometimes violent ones—on the South's railroads.

From time to time, black plaintiffs took the railroad companies to court and even won an occasional lawsuit. The courts generally ruled that railroads could segregate passengers, but only if they provided equal accommodations. In 1896, the United States Supreme Court validated what became known as the "separate but equal" doctrine in the case of *Plessy v. Ferguson*. In 1892, Adolph Plessy had been arrested for refusing to leave the white coach of a Louisiana train. He sued the railroad company, insisting on his right to travel in a first-class car on payment of a first-class fare. Railroads could not discriminate solely on the basis of skin color, Plessy argued, citing the Fourteenth Amendment.

The high court disagreed. "In the nature of things," the court ruled, the amendment "could not have been intended to abolish distinctions based upon color, or to enforce social, as distinguished from political equality."[14] There racial matters stood, separate but almost never equal, for the next half-century.

The 1890s saw the virtual elimination of Southern blacks from politics. Again, Mississippi took the lead. In fact, in an allusion to the redemption by violent means of 1874–75, the state's scheme to suppress the African-American vote became known as the "Second Mississippi Plan." Though 15 years of fraud and violence had sharply reduced the level of black political activity, six blacks still served in the state legislature in 1890. Blacks held a number of minor local offices as well, mostly by consent of the Democrats. Still, few whites would accept even limited black participation in public life.

John Lynch continued to wage his lonely, futile campaigns in Mississippi. In 1889, when the Republican Party returned to power nationally with the election of Benjamin Harrison to the presidency, Lynch tried to revive the party of Lincoln in his home state. Under Lynch's direction, the Republicans put together a full ticket for the first time since 1875, with an African-American candidate for secretary of state. Democrats turned furiously on Lynch and his small band of allies, eventually forcing the withdrawal of the entire ticket.

For many whites, the rewriting of state constitutions offered a foolproof method of denying blacks the vote, assuming that suppression clauses could be crafted in such a way as to meet federal tests of constitutionality. A lot of Southerners, it seemed, had seen enough of election-year lawbreaking. "I told them to go to it, boys, count them out," Alabama ex-governor William C. Oates admitted. "But we have gone from bad to worse until it has become a great evil. White men have gotten to cheating each other until we don't have any honest elections." Many another Southerner felt the sharp sting of conscience. In May 1890, Colonel B. F. Jones

White populist politicians used appeals to racial prejudice to overthrow the conservative leadership of the post–Civil War South. Benjamin R. ("Pitchfork Ben") Tillman addresses South Carolina farmers on October 12, 1904. (Library of Congress)

expressed what appears to have been a widely held view in a letter to the *Jackson Clarion-Ledger*:

> The old men of the present generation can't afford to die and leave their children with shotguns in their hands, a lie in their mouths and perjury on their souls. The constitution can be made so this will not be necessary.[15]

Lynch made essentially the same point. "If the negroes were disenfranchised according to the forms of law," he wrote, "there would be no occasion to suppress their votes by violence because they would have no votes to suppress; and having no votes in the ballot boxes, there would be no occasion to commit fraud in the count or perjury in the returns."[16] As one white Republican noted, the remedy for fraud dealt out further punishment to those who already had been injured. Even so, every state of the old Confederacy took steps to deprive blacks of the vote.

The new Mississippi constitution prescribed educational and property qualifications as well as a poll tax. It also contained a novel provision: the so-called "understanding clause." In order to qualify, a prospective voter needed to prove he could read and understand a section of the state constitution.

Lynch predicted that the clause would work only one way. "It was plain to everyone that its purpose was to so evade the Fifteenth Amendment as to disenfranchise the illiterate voters of one race without disenfranchising those of the other," he said. But some whites did in fact keep away. The Mississippi Plan, a Louisianan noted, admiring its neatness, "reduces the electorate and places the political control of the State in the hands not of a minority of the voters alone, but of *the minority of the whites*."[17] As it turned out, less than 10 percent of voting-age Mississippi blacks qualified, while roughly two thirds of whites were eligible. The new constitution reduced Mississippi's potential electorate, white and black, from 257,000 to 76,000.

Throughout the South, black–white conflict became inextricably entwined with Populism, the great political protest movement of the 1890s. If Populists elsewhere were calling for more democracy, not less, Southern Populists were if anything more enthusiastic about voter suppression measures than old-line Democrats. In Mississippi and South Carolina, small farmers and hill-country whites challenged the conservative political leadership of the long-established planter and professional classes of the Black Belt. But white supremacy was never at stake. In historian C. Vann Woodward's phrase, "The real question was *which whites* should be supreme."[18]

In South Carolina, Benjamin R. ("Pitchfork Ben") Tillman and his exclusively white upcountry followers campaigned for better schools, tax reform, and other progressive measures in seeking to overthrow the state's entrenched Democratic leadership. Yet it was Tillman who framed the understanding clause in the new state constitution of 1895 that effectively drove blacks out of politics. He offered no apology for his work:

> Some have said there is fraud in this understanding clause. Some poisons in small doses are very salutary and valuable medicines. There is no particle of fraud or illegality in it. It is just simply showing partiality, perhaps (laughter), or discriminating. Ah, you grin.[19]

Robert Smalls, one of only six black delegates to the constitutional convention, doubtless found Tillman's smirking defense of the clause galling in the extreme. Another white delegate put the matter bluntly. "We don't propose to have any fair elections," he told Smalls. "We will get left every time."[20] Understanding clauses, poll taxes, and property requirements, rather than Red Shirts and ballot fraud, would guarantee white dominion.

Repression bred bitterness and stoked blacks' anger. "We must and will have our day," a Selma, Alabama newspaper editor wrote, addressing whites. "You now have yours. You have had your revolutions, your civil wars and we here predict that at no very distant day we will have our race war, and we hope, as God intends, that we will be strong enough to wipe you out of existence and hardly leave enough of you to tell the story."[21]

Blacks joined the westward migration to escape new forms of social and economic oppression in the post–Reconstruction South. Some, such as the famous black cowboy Nat Love (also known as "Deadwood Dick"), found freedom in the wide-open spaces. (Library of Congress)

Still, lacking powerful allies, African Americans managed to mount only a feeble counter attack on Jim Crow Laws, though civil rights lawsuits, boycotts, and even labor strikes were sometimes successful. For some, the response was migration. The "Exoduster" movement developed in the mid-1870s when thousands of blacks, conceding the failure of Reconstruction, set out for homestead lands in Kansas and Nebraska. The Back to Africa movement held strong appeal, too. "If it is a negro country and we can be free and speak our own mind and make our own laws then we are ready to come at once," said Arkansan B. T. Willis in a letter to the African Colonization Society.[22] For most blacks, though, movement was impractical. The majority, denied a political voice and mired in poverty, had to endure conditions as best they could.

As the century neared its end, many Americans, white and black, acknowledged Booker T. Washington as the chief spokesman for black aspirations. Born into slavery in Virginia in 1856, an 1875 graduate of the Hampton Institute, Washington became principal of the Tuskegee Institute in 1881 and built it into perhaps the most powerful black institution in the country. From this platform, he spoke forcefully for vocational education as the key to black economic progress.

Washington set out his vision of racial peace in a famous speech at the Cotton States and International Exposition in Atlanta in September 1895. Looking out over a sea of mostly white faces, the only black on the speakers' platform, Washington felt a great responsibility and a tremendous sense of the occasion. "It was only a few years before that time," he mused, "that any white man in the audience might have claimed me as his slave."[23] He went on to deliver his influential "Atlanta Compromise" speech in which he claimed that blacks were more interested in industrial education and economic opportunity than in political and social rights.

Tennessee cabinetmaker Benjamin ("Pap") Singleton recruited thousands of blacks for the Kansas migration of the late 1870s. Singleton's converts were part of the "Exoduster" movement. (Kansas State Historical Society)

Patience and hard work would eventually overcome all obstacles. "It is at the bottom of life we must begin, and not at the top," Washington told his Atlanta audience. "Nor should we permit our grievances to overshadow our opportunities." In effect, he urged African Americans to suffer in silence, to accept political reality, and to quietly prepare for the day when full citizenship would be granted them. He went on:

> The wisest among my race understand that the agitation of questions of social equality is the extremest folly, and that progress in the enjoyment of all the privileges that will come to us must be the result of severe and constant struggle rather than of artificial forcing. It is important and right that all privileges of the law be ours, but it is vastly more important that we be prepared for the exercise of these privileges.[24]

Washington willingly accommodated Southern conservatives on the racial questions of the day. He did not object to literacy and property qualifications for the ballot as long as they were applied to both races. (They were not.) He even seemed to accept the idea of segregation, at least for the time being, arguing that deep-rooted racial antipathies could take decades to eradicate. "These prejudices are something that it does not pay to disturb," Washington warned.[25] Many whites, Northern and Southern, embraced Washington's Atlanta Compromise as a potential way out of the racial impasse. But his views deeply alienated some African Americans, especially the rising class of black intellectuals.

William Edward Burghardt DuBois, historian, political activist, and author, emerged as Washington's most persistent critic. Born in 1868 in Great Barrington, Massachusetts and educated at Fisk University and Harvard, he called for an activist political role for blacks. DuBois challenged Washington's emphasis on vocational training, believing that a

Search for a Zion

With the collapse of the Reconstruction governments and the triumph of reaction, significant numbers of Southern blacks began to search for an escape. For a comparative few, emigration to the West African nation of Liberia seemed to offer an answer. For many thousands more in the late 1870s, Kansas beckoned.

Prominent black leaders, Frederick Douglass among them, opposed migration, arguing that it suggested surrender in the struggle for civil rights in the post-Reconstruction South. But Douglass did not live in Tennessee, Mississippi, Louisiana, or Texas, the states from which thousands of freed people set out in quest of land, schools, political rights, and freedom from white terror.

In Tennessee, the elderly former slave Benjamin "Pap" Singleton established a land agency to resettle blacks in Kansas. A cabinetmaker by trade, Singleton fled to Canada before the Civil War and later lived in Detroit, where he ran a boardinghouse that catered to escaped slaves. He returned to Nashville after the war. Among other carpentry jobs, he made coffins for black people killed in Reconstruction-era political violence.

liberally educated black middle class offered the best hope for progress.

DuBois broke openly with Washington in the late 1890s, risking retribution from the "Tuskegee machine"—Washington's powerful network of connections. A word from Washington, who controlled Northern sources of charitable funding, could make or break a struggling black institution such as Atlanta University, where DuBois taught from 1896 to 1910. Few black political appointments were made anywhere, in the North or the South, without Washington's consent. Nevertheless, DuBois, angry, articulate, more the poet than the politician, challenged the colossus.

From the mid-1870s, Singleton preached migration as a way out. He organized meetings, published circulars, and bought advertisements in newspapers promoting the migration scheme. "Ho for Kansas!" one of his circulars shouted, and thousands of black Tennesseans responded. "I am the cause of the Kansas immigration," Singleton claimed.[28]

In fact, Singleton had little to do with the remarkable mass movement of blacks into Kansas in the spring of 1879. In a spontaneous rush, some 6,000 African Americans—the Exodusters—poured northward out of Mississippi, Louisiana, and Texas.

By 1880, 15,000 blacks had resettled in Kansas. They had not, however, discovered a prairie paradise. Free lands were not available for the taking, as many migrants had believed. Most worked as laborers or domestics. Some were able eventually to save enough money to buy land, though. And even for laboring people, conditions were easier. Wages were better. Kansas offered basic political rights. Blacks were safe from the casual racial violence that continued to be a feature of life in the former Confederate states.

Most blacks, of course, stayed home, unwilling to leave familiar places behind, to sever ties with those who had been born, lived, and died before them. As one freedman explained his attachments:

"We feel sorry to think we have to leave our fathers, mothers, wives and children's dust, and flee into other states to make a living."[29] ◆

Near the end of his long life (he died in 1963), DuBois offered this summary of his turn-of-the-century quarrel with Washington:

At a time when Negro civil rights called for organized and aggressive defense, he broke down that defense by advising acquiescence or at least no open agitation. During the period when laws disenfranchising the Negro were being passed in all the Southern states, and when these laws were being supplemented by "jim crow" travel laws and other enactments making color caste legal, his public speeches tended continually to excuse it, to emphasize the shortcomings of the Negro, and were widely interpreted as putting the chief onus for his condition on the Negro himself.[26]

DuBois inspired the Niagara Movement, which demanded for blacks "every single right that belongs to the freeborn American, political, civil and social." These were words of near-revolutionary import in 1905, when DuBois and his allies launched the movement. To many observers, the mass of blacks seemed to have made negligible progress since Reconstruction. "The rights of the Negroes are at a lower ebb than at any time during the thirty-five years of their freedom, and the race prejudice more intense and uncompromising," the author Charles Chesnutt had written only two years before.[27] Truly, in these first years of the new century, Rufus Saxton's brilliant day of promise seemed buried deep in the past.

NOTES

1. Leslie Fishel, Jr. and Benjamin Quarles, *The Black American: A Documentary History* (New York: William Morrow & Company, 1970), 305.

2. Joel Williamson, *After Slavery: The Negro in South Carolina during Reconstruction, 1861–1877* (Chapel Hill: University of North Carolina Press, 1965), 415.

3. Vernon L. Wharton, *The Negro in Mississippi: 1865–1900* (New York: Harper & Row, 1965), 202.

4. Eric Foner, *Reconstruction: America's Unfinished Revolution, 1863–1877* (New York: Harper & Row, 1988), 589.

5. Willie Lee Rose, *Rehearsal for Reconstruction: The Port Royal Experiment* (Indianapolis: Bobbs, Merrill, 1964), 384.

6. Wharton, *The Negro in Mississippi*, 67.

7. Edward L. Ayers, *The Promise of the New South: Life after Reconstruction* (New York: Oxford University Press, 1992), 200.

8. Ayers, *Promise of the New South*, 430.

9. Ayers, *Promise of the New South*, 209.

10. Ayers, *Promise of the New South*, 195.

11. Ayers, *Promise of the New South*, 153.

12. W. E. B. DuBois, *Black Reconstruction in America* (New York: Russell & Russell, 1962), 30.

13. Ayers, *Promise of the New South*, 139.

14. Rembert W. Patrick, *Reconstruction of the Nation* (New York: Oxford University Press, 1967), 297.

15. First quote, C. Vann Woodward, *The Origins of the New South: 1877–1913* (Baton Rouge: Louisiana State University Press, 1971 ed.), 326; second quote, Wharton, *The Negro in Mississippi*, 207.

16. John Roy Lynch, *Reminiscences of an Active Life*, John Hope Franklin, ed. (Chicago: University of Chicago Press, 1970), 342.

17. First quote, Lynch, *Reminiscences*, 341; second quote, Woodward, *Origins of the New South*, 336.

18. Woodward, *Origins of the New South*, 328.

19. Woodward, *Origins of the New South*, 333.

20. Rose, *Rehearsal for Reconstruction*, 404.

21. Ayers, *Promise of the New South*, 145.

22. Ayers, *Promise of the New South*, 429.

23. Booker T. Washington, *Up from Slavery* (Garden City, N.Y.: Doubleday, 1901), 211.

24. Washington, *Up from Slavery*, 220, 223–24.

25. Woodward, *Origins of the New South*, 357.

26. W. E. B. DuBois, *The Autobiography of W. E. B. DuBois* (New York: International Publishers, 1968), 238.

27. Woodward, *Origins of the New South*, 368, 355.

28. Nell Irvin Painter, *Exodusters: Black Migration to Kansas after Reconstruction* (New York: Alfred A. Knopf, 1977), 108.

29. Painter, *Exodusters*, 113.

EPILOGUE:
1913 *and After*

In 1865, early in the journey from slavery to freedom, the educator and author Lydia Maria Child advised the freed people to make the most of what little they could call their own. "Whitewash is not expensive," she noted, "and it takes but little time to transplant a cherokee rose, a jessamine, or other wild shrubs and vines, that make the poorest cabin look beautiful."[1] By 1913, thousands of African Americans, starting with nothing, had built rich lives. They formed stable families, a condition denied them during slavery. They learned to read and write: learning had been a crime for blacks in the prewar South. They established political, social, and religious institutions. No such organizations had been permitted to exist under slavery. They ran farms and businesses and became doctors and lawyers and teachers.

Blacks celebrated the year of the Jubilee in 1913, the 50th anniversary of President Lincoln's Emancipation Proclamation. Commemorative events and expositions all over the South hailed the advances of five decades. Illiteracy had fallen to around 30 percent from more than 90 percent in 1865. Blacks owned 128,557 farms in 1913. They owned 38,000 businesses. They owned 550,000 homes.

Sea Islander Robert Smalls, born in 1839, could remember a time when masters could abuse their slaves on a whim. "My aunt," he once told an interviewer, "was whipped so many a time until she has not the same skin she was born with."[2] Smalls had lived a full, varied life since he steered the *Planter* out of Charleston harbor in 1862. He had taught himself to read and write. He had made money as a merchant. For many years, until whites finally drove him from politics, Smalls reigned as the all-powerful political king of Beaufort, South Carolina. He lived out his last years with a patronage job, a federal appointment as collector of the port of Beaufort. Smalls died in 1915.

Still, as the historian C. Vann Woodward has pointed out, the statistics on land and business ownership, and individual triumphs such as Smalls's or Booker T. Washington's, represent the achievements of a comparatively small black middle class. For the mass of African Americans, poverty, deprivation, lack of opportunity, and political, social, and economic oppression were basic facts of existence.

And racism in America was as pervasive as ever. In 1890, a group of prominent white and black leaders met in upstate New York for a "Conference on the Negro Question." There was a lot of earnest talk. But the remark of one participant, a white carpetbagger and former judge named Albion Tourgée, reflected reality in a way none of the speeches, however well-meaning, had managed to do. There is no "negro problem," Tourgée said. "The hate, the oppression, the injustice, are all on our own side."[3] In that regard, things had changed little by the year of the Jubilee.

"Caste is the curse of the world," Adelbert Ames, the carpetbagger governor of Mississippi, wrote to former Mississippi congressman John Roy Lynch in 1914.[4] Post-Reconstruction Mississippi proved more than Lynch, born enslaved, could abide. He finally abandoned his efforts to revive the Republican Party and moved north, to Washington and Chicago, where he held a succession of minor government offices and wrote a series of passionate defenses of Reconstruction-era politics.

In 1913, Lynch published a rebuttal to the school of historical writing that, from the 1890s, had portrayed Reconstruction regimes as barbaric and corrupt. "I do not hesitate to assert that the Southern Reconstruction governments were the best governments those states ever had," he wrote in *The Facts of Reconstruction.*[5]

White intransigence brought those governments down, and white supremacist rule imposed a caste system nearly as rigid as any the South had known in slavery times. By the 1890s, blacks by the thousands were fleeing the stricken fields of the rural South. The black population of Southern cities increased by 32 percent in the 1890s and by 36 percent in the first decade of the 20th century. By 1910, too, many thousands had followed John Lynch's lead and migrated north, where at least a semblance of equity might be found, and where at least the chance at a decent living might be had. The great black diaspora had begun.

African Americans continued to be denied a political voice in the South. In the 1930s, when the Great Depression spread mass social and economic distress across America, the civil rights movement began to regain its strength. Those fighting for black rights could take comfort in the single most important legacy of the Reconstruction era: the Fourteenth and Fifteenth Amendments, which guaranteed due process and equality before the law. The amendments established a legal framework for true black emancipation, and they remained on the books. In the long reach, they ensured that Reconstruction, for all its failures, omissions, and ambiguities, would be an enduring achievement.

During the Depression, Northern radicals journeyed south to organize black farmworkers. Though they met with indifferent success, they proved to be the advance guard of the legions of civil rights workers, Northern blacks as well as whites, who would fan out over the South in the 1950s and

1960s to challenge and finally dismantle the post-Reconstruction system of white supremacy.

"The [Northerners] came down to bring emancipation and left before it was over," Alabama sharecropper Ned Cobb, thinking of the Yankee armies of the Civil War, said in the 1930s. "Now they've come to finish the job."[6]

NOTES

1. Lydia Maria Child, *The Freedmen's Book* (New York: Arno Press, 1968 reprint), 271.

2. John W. Blassingame, ed., *Slave Testimony* (Baton Rouge: Louisiana State University Press, 1977), 379.

3. Eric Foner, *Reconstruction: America's Unfinished Revolution, 1863–1877* (New York: Harper & Row, 1988), 606.

4. Foner, *Reconstruction*, 609.

5. John Roy Lynch, *The Facts of Reconstruction* (New York: Arno Press, 1968 reprint), 33.

6. Foner, *Reconstruction*, 611.

Index

Boldface numbers indicate major topics.
Italic numbers indicate illustrations.
Numbers followed by m indicate maps.

graft. *See* corruption
Grant, Ulysses S.   21, 25, 28, 33, 34, 67, 86–87, 99, 113, 114, 116, 117, 121
Great Depression   148
Greene County (Ala.)   110

H

Hampton, Wade   **118–21**, 123, 128
Hampton (Va.)   38, 39
Hancock, Cornelia   69
Harrison, Benjamin   134
Hayes, Rutherford B.   121, 122, 124
Haywood, Felix   34
Henry, Sam   111
Higginson, Thomas Wentworth   16–17, 61
Hilton Head (S.C.)   7–8, 13
Holmes, Benjamin   102
Homestead Act   96
Howard, Oliver Otis   45, 64
Howard University   131
Hughes, Margaret   24
Humphries, Benjamin G.   63
Hunter, David   13, 14

I

Illiteracy   39–40, 146

J

Jackson, A. N.   132
Jackson (Miss.)   114, 133
Jay Gould and Company   102
Jim Crow laws   133, 139
Johnson, Andrew   44, 61–64, 66–69, 72–74, 77–80, 82–86, *83*
Johnson, Henry   94
Joint Committee on Reconstruction   73–74
Jones, B. F.   134–135
Julian, George   78
justice system   *55*, 130

K

Kansas   139   142–143
Kellogg, William P.   117
Ku Klux Klan   86, 109, 110, 118, 123

L

labor
    army   25–27
    contracts   32, **47–49**, 65, 66–67, 68, 97, 129–130
    free   10–11
    idleness   49–50
    during Reconstruction   79–80, 96–97
land   60–61, 64
    distribution   30–31, 61, *96*, 109